The
ATH____
in YOU

Kinta Kadakia Patel

PRAISE FOR THE AUTHOR

'During the time I played, sports nutrition was not taken too seriously. But with the game becoming professional and multi-formatted, today's players understand the importance of fitness and nutrition. You can't have one without the other. I am glad that Kinita, a one-of-a-kind sports nutritionist, has come out with a book that explains in easy language why sports nutrition is needed for a fit body and to enjoy sport'

—**Sunil Gavaskar, former Indian cricketer**

'We can find all sorts of excuses—"I have no time," "I don't have the expertise," "My long work hours prevent me from maintaining a healthy lifestyle"—for not taking that first step towards a healthy body. Working with Kinita allowed me to match my training programme with her well-balanced nutritional plan, and this allowed me to achieve my goal of peak performance. With Kinita's forty-day body transformation plan, I was able to achieve maximum results, despite being on the road and facing the challenges of ever-changing meal options and timings'

—**Jonty Rhodes, former cricketer**

'Over years of playing cricket I have realized the positive impact of fitness training and good nutrition not only on my performance but also on my overall physique and stamina. Kinita, through this book, is trying to spread the same message'

—**Harbhajan Singh, Indian cricketer; and former captain of Punjab state team and IPL team Mumbai Indians**

'Kinita, along with being a great sports nutritionist, also has a silently motivating spirit. She's on the journey with you, every step of the way. Her nutrition methods for a demanding sport like cricket, where no one game is like the other, helps one recover, play and perform at their best'

—**Krunal Pandya and Hardik Pandya, cricketers, Mumbai Indians and the Indian cricket team respectively**

'What sets Kinita apart from other nutritionists is her up-to-date knowledge in the ever-evolving field of sports nutrition. Her patience, hard work and passion through the crucial months of the IPL has benefited the players of the Mumbai Indians team tremendously'

—**Rahul Sanghvi, former Indian cricketer and team manager, Mumbai Indians**

'I remember when I met Kinita, I was 78 kilos and in less than three months, I was down to 66 kilos. The best part about this journey of weight loss was that I was not dieting; I was only eating the right things at the right time and working out as per a plan made in consultation with Kinita and the fitness trainer. I was able to train and focus better because I never felt lazy or lethargic. The fat to muscle ratio in my body improved significantly and I have never been as fit. The best part about Kinita is her patience and belief in her clients. She always listened to me and gave me food to eat as per my preferences and schedule. She also explained why I needed to include certain foods and reduce the intake of others, thereby increasing my intrinsic motivation and desire to do what is right and resist temptation. Hence, it was easy to implement and execute her plans. She maintained records systematically, so we had all the data—what I ate, what my workout and intensity were like, what my results were in terms of performance in my sport—and we were moving in a direction, as opposed to just losing weight without checking if it was helping in my performance or not. She is a thorough professional and a master at her work'
—Ronak Pandit, gold medallist and record holder in the 2006 Commonwealth Games; Asian champion and Asian record holder; current coach to Olympians (London 2012 and Rio 2016 Olympics); and world record holder in shooting

'Kinita is a highly regarded sports nutritionist, and her knowledge and expertise have been integral in enhancing the high-performance cricket programmes in which she has been involved. Kinita's professionalism and ability to understand the need of athletes to perform, combined with her knowledge of Indian and international cuisine, makes her the Indian expert'
—Paul Chapman, strength and conditioning coach for Cricket NSW and Mumbai Indians

'In this world of many illogical diet trends, Kinita is a refreshing change. Being a sports nutritionist, she understands the importance of muscle gain for fat loss, which most dieticians today don't. Unlike others, she encourages her clients to exercise or play sports. She also explains the importance of resistance training to achieve a fit, toned body over a thin, slim one. And that's why I love her'
—Yasmin Karachiwala, Pilates master trainer and celebrity fitness trainer

'Kinita is full of life, bubbly, helpful, knowledgeable and always up to the mark with her work. The best in the business that I have come across in sports nutrition'
—Deanne Panday, fitness author and holistic lifestyle coach

'I know Kinita for over a decade now. Her in-depth knowledge on nutrition and her options for different foods make her method really easy to understand and follow. Without cheating, I have seen great results, coupled with smiles running from one ear to the other. I have heard her talk about her subject with so much passion that it changed my perspective about food for the better. It helped me to improve and recover my patients' muscle strength much better post surgery and post injury'
—Dr Hemakshi Basu, sports physiotherapist

'I have known Kinita for fifteen years now, and what stands out is her dedication to her profession. In the constantly evolving scientific world of sports nutrition, she has kept abreast of cutting-edge knowledge in the field. This, coupled with the ability to understand the individual needs of her clients, makes her excellent at her work'
—Dr Aashish Contractor, head of department, Rehabilitation and Sports Medicine, Sir H.N. Reliance Foundation Hospital, Mumbai

'Kinita's dietary advice is very easy to follow as it is incorporated into one's daily schedule. She has successfully helped many of my patients with obesity and PCOS, reducing the amount of medications they need. On a personal note, I fondly call her "Kadakbai" as she is strict in her demeanour, but charmingly inspires you to follow her food plan'
—Dr Avan Dadina, gynaecologist

'I feel Kinita's diet affects your body not only from the outside but also from within because her diet is all about complete nutrition'
—Jimmy Shergill, Bollywood actor

'Working with Kinita has not only changed my body type but has brought with it clarity, flexibility, practicality and the joy of eating well. I know how much and what to eat and at what times, which helps me adapt to changing situations and travel plans. Also, especially since my work entails facing the camera, a planned, appropriate diet for a lean look at all times is a must. This was possible only after I started consulting with Kinita. Movie making is more interesting and fulfilling as now I can look my best without starving and depending on the impractical diets that otherwise sell in the market. Kudos to Kinita and more power to you'

—Tusshar Kapoor, Bollywood actor

'Kinita is the reason for my physical well-being. I am grateful to her for her help as nothing else has helped me as she has'

—Neila Shammi Kapoor

'Through her nutrition plans, great results are always guaranteed! I never look pale, I'm never left feeling hungry, my skin glows and I just end up feeling super. She's my favourite nutritionist'

— Bhavana C. Pandey, entrepreneur

'Her approach to nutrition and healthy eating busts the myth that food that's good for you is boring or hard to follow. Her approach offers practical solutions, which is why it's effective. Oh, and don't be fooled by that pretty face—she's quite the task master'

—Priya Tanna, editor, *Vogue India*

'I'm addicted to Kinita. She lets me eat all my favourite food. I never feel like I'm on a diet. The best part is that I'm never hungry or starving. Her mantra is "eat till you are full", which works very well for me as I hate being told specific quantities. She's the best nutritionist we have'

—Dolly R. Sidhwani, partner, Noble Faith; and director,
Love Generation

'"It's like you are permanently carrying a 15-kilo carry-on" . . . That line stuck in my brain. She is gentle yet firm, and patiently keeps trying till she finds the right fix for you. Then magic! Now I can knock off 3 or 4 kilos easily and maintain my weight. She taught me how to eat and live sensibly . . . A star angel'

—Ashok Kurien, founder–promoter/director, Zee Entertainment
Enterprises Ltd and Ambience Advertising Pvt. Ltd

'Your nutrition guidance and support did tremendous work in shaping me and helping me run better. I admired your work for many reasons—your simple approach to understand my needs and existing diet. You did not make any drastic changes that did not suit my taste. You explained to me the pros and cons in detail, so that I was not forced into anything blindly and instead accepted the facts using logic. Obviously, the effect is better this way. Your depth of knowledge for

the Indian diet helped me adapt to changes within my traditional, regional taste. Above all, you are a fantastic and pleasing person to meet. Keep making positive changes in the lives of people. I sincerely convey my gratitude for your support as it was after I sought your guidance in 2013 that I clocked my best timing in a half marathon'
—Major D.P. Singh, Indian blade runner; Limca record holder; and founder, The Challenging Ones

'Six months after my second pregnancy, I felt the need to get my energy levels up, get into shape and follow a suitable diet. Taking care of both my kids—Deanne, 4, and Mikhail, 6 months, at that time— was exhausting, and so I went to Kinita. She understood how much I loved my food and how, at the same time, my work and taking care of my kids required me to stay fit and healthy. She recommended food options and an exercise routine that I could follow. The process was slow and steady, and within a few months I noticed a big change, and before I knew it, I was 10 to 12 kilos lighter'
—Parizad Kolah Marshall, model and television host

'Kinita's plan is a way of life, and her energy and passion behind it makes you want to listen. The amount of food she assigned was unbelievable. I loved the feeling of being full and satisfied from nutritious, healthy food, yet seeing the weight drop on the scale'
—Renu R. Chopra, B.R. Films

'Kinita understands the needs of amateur yet serious runners in a very unique manner. I have referred to nutritionists before, but most focused on weight loss, which resulted in energy loss through the day. Within months of setting my objectives of weight loss, controlling cramps and meeting energy requirements through the working day and through long runs, I managed to achieve what I had desired without it ever seeming very difficult. Her ever-changing diet is an apt formula for nutrition, which is practical and sustainable over an extended period, till it comfortably becomes a lifestyle. Thanks to her, I achieved my full- (personal best 3:47) and half-marathon (personal best 1:38) milestones over the last two years and even more importantly, have higher energy than most colleagues at work at 7 p.m.'
—Gagan Banga, vice chairman and MD, Indiabulls Housing Finance Ltd

'I honestly wish Kinita had come into my life earlier and provided me with her magical solution: a very special diet that was created for me. And mind you, all throughout, I never felt like I was on a diet as she would give me plenty to eat. With her, it was like a "gain" and "lose" situation. I "lost" the weight and "gained" my confidence, for which I am eternally grateful to her. I still follow her diet principles and have managed to maintain my weight loss'

—Pallavi Jaikishan, designer

'Kinita's dedication and knowledge is inspiring. She motivated me and was not just my nutritionist but my friend and confidante. She always made me feel comfortable and yet, was aware of my need to eat sensibly and change my thinking on the right food combinations . . . and of course, exercise! Kinita is a lovely, positive person who empowered me to change my life towards positive, healthy living'

—Isha Mehra, designer

'A pure combination of a lovely, nice and beautiful person, who gives a lot to eat to lose weight. The best part about this is that one actually succeeds by doing so. The happiness goes unnoticed'

—Sabrina Jani, works with Abu Jani Sandeep Khosla

The
ATHLETE
in YOU

A guide to eating, playing and
performing like an athlete

KINITA KADAKIA PATEL

EBURY
PRESS

EBURY PRESS

USA | Canada | UK | Ireland | Australia
New Zealand | India | South Africa | China

Ebury Press is part of the Penguin Random House group of companies
whose addresses can be found at global.penguinrandomhouse.com

Published by Penguin Random House India Pvt. Ltd
7th Floor, Infinity Tower C, DLF Cyber City,
Gurgaon 122 002, Haryana, India

First published in Ebury Press by Penguin Random House India 2016

ISBN 9788184007091

Typeset in GoudyOlSt BT by Manipal Digital Systems, Manipal
Printed at Thomson Press India Ltd, New Delhi

www.penguinbooksindia.com

In warm and heartfelt memory of my father,
truly one in a million.
I miss you.

CONTENTS

PART IV: SUPPLEMENTS

PART V: SPORTS TRAINING

PART VI: LIVE, EAT AND COOK LIKE AN ATHLETE

PART VII: A YEAR OF EVENTS

PART VIII: INJURIES AND INJURY PREVENTION

INTRODUCTION

Welcome to what I hope will be a life-transforming book for you. But before I go any further, I want to make one thing clear: this is NOT a 'weight loss' book or a 'diet' book or an 'exercise' book. I am not an exercise or diet guru, and by no means is this book trying to validate either of these things. This book is based on my personal experience of viewing exercise as a sport and diet as nutrition. I strongly believe that a sportsperson, whether a professional or an amateur, is a phenomenal individual with a strongly focused mind, a fit body and a positively competitive soul.

This book is going to help you become exactly this person. It will help you be like an athlete, eat like an athlete and think like an athlete. In short, it will help you take up athleticism as your new religion.

Globally today an athletic body is considered the most attractive by a vast majority of the population. Gone are the days when runway thin models were the 'in' look or when men needed to have bodybuilder physiques. This is great news because the athletic body is a much healthier body image to strive for. However, this goal is very different from the average body of today's individual, who tends to have narrow shoulders due to lack of muscle mass and a larger waistline due to extra fat, along with thinner legs in men or larger legs in women (since women tend to naturally store fat in the hip and thigh regions).

On a daily basis, I see people who are frustrated and struggling with their health, body image, and overall well-being. You too are likely in this position, which is why you picked up this book in the first place. I promise you, you will not regret the decision to move to an athletic lifestyle. The great news is that if you are ready to create change in your life, you are in for some serious benefits.

Let me begin by sharing my own story. Like many others, I too was once overweight and had no clue on how to begin losing weight. At sixteen, I realized the excess weight came with low self-esteem and the emotional baggage of wanting to be accepted respectfully in society. When I should have been having fun with friends and eating tubs of popcorn at movies, I was battling my inner self. I knew that I wasn't as healthy as I could be. It was at this point that I decided to do something about it, and all I had on my side was my mental strength and the determination to achieve my target.

I made a start and took up running. I ran on roads that never seemed to end. I covered distances I never thought I could. It felt great and I loved how athletic it made me feel. Soon after, I decided to take up swimming as well. My love for physical activity only continued to grow and I never looked back. I was always interested in seeing new training techniques come out and giving it a try in my personal fitness programme.

During this time, I was also busy pursuing the education I needed to eventually work in this field. I studied nutrition and went on to do a masters' degree in it. Understanding how the right foods could be used to fuel my body for all of my athletic endeavours made all the difference to my life. Now that I was eating right, exercising regularly and feeling healthier than ever, I was able to lose 15 kilograms and completely transform my body.

Why You Should Read This Book

Wonderful things happen when you start to look after your body and eating the way you need to, for your health first and foremost. Too many people rush out on a weight loss diet plan that robs the body of the nutrients it needs to be healthy as well as the energy it needs to exercise.

The end result is a body that's getting smaller but weaker. This is not a wise goal to strive for. Instead, strive to eat in a way that makes you stronger, helps you melt fat but still build lean muscle mass so you become fitter, toned and get a strong, athletic look. Being 'thin' or 'skinny' is no longer the 'in' thing. Going on fad diets and losing weight will only make you look sick, not fit. By all means, attain your desired size zero if that's your goal, but not with a diet. Do it with a good nutrition plan and an athletic regime.

If being fit is what you're interested in, you've come to the right place because that's exactly what I'm going to show you how to do over the course of this book. As you read this book, picture yourself carrying out these changes in your life. I hope you use this information, not just read it and stop there.

Remember, positive changes will only come if you take action in your daily life. If you're ready, then let's get straight to it.

PART I

DEFINING AN ATHLETE

This book is all about a single word: the athlete. We all are athletes in our own spaces, living and fighting to achieve the best for ourselves. But what we need is to compete with our lifestyles and focus on becoming a fitter, healthier and more athletic individual. Let's understand what an athlete is and how you can become one.

1

WHO IS AN ATHLETE?

When you hear the term 'athlete', what comes to your mind?

For many people, thoughts of hours spent training, incredible hard work and unparalleled dedication enters their mind. For others, they visualize a well-built, muscular, lean and agile body. Whatever particular ideas come to your mind when you hear the word, there's no denying that athletes strive to be fit, strong and most often, are positively conscious about their body image, which, though aesthetically pleasing in a way, helps them with their sport of choice.

While the average individual may choose to eat better and exercise for health and body image reasons, athletes choose to do so for performance-based reasons. They don't just want to look good, they want to perform optimally. In a manner of speaking, they are the Ferrari of the body kingdom.

Is this something you would like to see yourself as? Fit, toned, athletic? Now, the great news is that you don't have to quit your job and dedicate five hours of training daily to get an athletic body. You may not go on to compete in the Olympics unless you do some serious training, but if you wish to have an athletic body and reap many of the benefits that come with it, this book will show you how you can do so in just a few hours a week of exercise and sports training along with some smart nutrition.

One thing that some people overlook when it comes to athletes is how much importance they place on their nutrition. It's rare to see high-level athletes feasting on burgers and fries at a local fast-food joint. Unless, of course, they have just won a world championship and are celebrating their win. They know that if they want their body to run at optimum performance levels, they need to be feeding themselves nothing but optimum food sources.

If you put low-grade petrol in a sports car, it won't drive like it should. It's the same concept with your body. To really obtain a physique like an athlete's, you need to marry proper training with smart nutrition. Note that I did not say exercise along with diet here. Smart athletes do not *diet*. The word 'diet' in the current context implies that you are taking something away from your body—you are living on less than you need. This is not what you want. Instead, you actually want to feed your body *more* of the proper foods, which will then help you naturally take care of your weight. When coupled with the right physical training, weight loss happens almost automatically with no strict calorie counting required.

Does all of this sound complicated? Don't worry, it doesn't have to be. I'm going to make things as simple as possible so that you can easily move forward and achieve the more athletic lifestyle that you desire.

If you pick out any diet book at random, chances are that you'll find a plan that often leaves the body nutritionally deficient, with a sluggish metabolic rate (when the diet is followed long enough), and a loss of lean muscle mass. If you lose muscle while on a diet, think of yourself as moving backwards. It's one of the worst outcomes that could occur since it is your lean muscle mass tissue that helps you stay strong while burning fat to keep you at a healthy body weight.

Athletes pride themselves on gaining muscle, so the last thing they want is to lose it. Yet, any traditional diet plan will put you at a high risk of doing just that. When it comes to athletic nutrition, becoming thinner is not the goal. Instead, you'll be focusing on achieving goals like:

- Obtaining a toned body
- Improving muscular strength and power
- Enhancing your aerobic capacity
- Increasing lean muscle
- Replenishing lost nutrients effectively to perform better
- Balancing your fluid and electrolyte levels for optimal physical performance and blood pressure
- Preventing and healing any resultant injuries
- Improving daily energy levels so that intense exercise can be undertaken

Above are the goals of a proper athletic programme that combines smart training with good nutrition and these are the very objectives that this book aims to help you achieve. Moreover, this book is going to help you become strong and fit—and incredibly proud of what your body can do.

2

A CLOSER LOOK AT THE BODY OF AN ATHLETE

When looking at the body of an athlete, it's easy to see why it's so desirable. Male athletes usually have broad shoulders that form a V-shape and taper into a narrow waist and hips, complemented by powerful legs. Female athletes also have that V-shaped appearance to a slight degree, which gives the impression of a streamlined waist and that hourglass figure that so many women covet. Female athletes who build muscle, despite what many women believe, do not end up looking bulky but rather, they tend to gain curves in their body in all the right places, giving them a feminine yet a strong appearance.

All these different body types can be classified based on somatotype, or the three main types of physical builds. These three types are endomorphs, ectomorphs and mesomorphs.

Look at the table below and understand the detailed characteristics of each type. You will be able to categorize yourself under one of the three. This is the first step towards attaining an athletic lifestyle. By spotting your body type, you will be able to select a sport and its complementing nutrition programme that will best suit you to help achieve your goal.

From this information, you can tell that the mesomorph somatotype is the most athletic in nature. Mesomorphs are natural athletes, the individuals who have always been good at sports. While these individuals may have it slightly easier when it comes to applying athletic training and nutrition to their lifestyles, it doesn't mean that endomorphs or ectomorphs cannot be successful athletes. It will just take a little more work and/or a precise game plan to get results.

Whether you are an athlete or a non-athlete, you are going to have a body type and this is something you cannot change. But while you cannot completely change your body type (go from an endomorph to an ectomorph for example), you can make your body more like another body type.

Take for instance if an endomorph, characterized as someone who puts on body fat easily with a tendency to have a round and robust shape, does regular weightlifting exercises and gets on a nutrition programme, they will build up more lean muscle mass. This will change their natural metabolic

Endomorph	Ectomorph	Mesomorph
• Gains body fat very easily	• Naturally very thin and straight looking	• Naturally very muscular
• Has a slow resting metabolic rate	• Is often quite tall	• Puts on quality lean weight without too much of a struggle
• Tends to store body fat in the midsection of the body	• Often has a fidgety personality (always has to be moving)	• Is highly athletic (typically the star athlete in school)
• Is not naturally very athletic	• Eats any kind of food without much weight gain	• Tends to excel at most physical activities
• Tends to be lazy and inactive	• May show signs of a low appetite	• May gain body fat due to eating poorly (but not as easily as an endomorph)
• Has little muscle mass	• Often excels at distance or endurance sports such as marathons	• Can lose body fat quite easily without too much effort
• Has a very hard time losing weight	• May be a highly stressed or a highly strung individual	• Tends to have a short and thick appearance
• The mere sight of food can cause weight gain		• Can also have a curvy appearance (for women)
• Has an aaple- or pear-shaped physique		• Can have a V-shaped appearance (for men)

tendencies and they will start to become a lot more like mesomorphs. So even while they are never going to be a pure mesomorph, their body will behave in a similar way, thanks to their training and food.

Heaving a sigh of relief after hearing this? The fact is you may need to struggle but you don't need to put up with your body the way it is for the rest of your life. Unfortunately, what many land up doing in their pursuit to lose weight is a regular diet and exercise programme, which will only (in the best-case scenario) turn you into a smaller version of your current self. What you need instead is a body type transformation. Those who complete full-body transformations usually adopt a more athletic approach to achieve this.

Well, then, coming back to the point, have you managed to classify yourself in a specific body type? Let's move ahead and understand a very important concept. The reason why we have spent so much time deciphering body types is that based on your somatotype, you will tend to excel at certain sports more than others and be drawn to that form of training. For instance, the ectomorph is the classic, long-distance running athlete. These individuals will be able to quickly succeed with their efforts in these sports compared to, for example, how well an endomorph might do. They also tend to be better at football, which also requires a high level of cardiovascular capacity thanks to the running involved. In contrast, a mesomorph, who tends to be short and stocky, will typically excel at sports such as sprinting, football and hockey. Both an ectomorph and endomorph can play racquet sports quite well and with the right training develop an ideal physique for the sport. Similarly, both individuals can make great swimmers depending on the nutrition and exercise. These athletes will have very strong, muscular shoulders while the rest of their body tends to be more streamlined, especially throughout the hip region. This helps them move quickly in water without much water resistance over the curves of their body. As you can see, this can be achieved with either the ectomorph or mesomorph body type quite easily.

The table below lists the sports that each body type tends to excel at:

Endomorph	Mesomorph	Ectomorph
Racquet sports	Hockey	Long-distance
Swimming	Football	running
Cycling	Sprinting	Football
Cricket	Track and field	Racquet sports
	sports	Swimming
	Swimming	

Endomorphs, comparatively, would struggle more to excel in the specific sport selected than the other somatotypes. To make sure they get results, the key is to lower the body fat levels as well as focusing on building lean mass. While an endomorph may not build muscle nearly as readily as, say, a mesomorph would, they can still build muscle with the right training. And when they do, they will be able to play all the same sports.

Very few endomorphs, however, will go on to do long-distance events such as marathons. Their body simply isn't made for this type of athletic event and training, and more often than not, they will not find it enjoyable at all. For an endomorph to become a long-distance runner, they would first require a body type transformation and sincere dedication towards this goal.

The type of training you do will dictate the way in which your body builds muscle and burns fat—whether it's to a higher degree of total mass all over your body or only additional muscle in regions where you need it the most. As this process takes place, it allows you to continue to excel at your sport of choice.

Another thing to note about athletic training is that most people who begin this type of training find that after a while, they are less focused on how their body looks and much more focused on what their body can do. This attitude helps shift the focus away from a negative body image and mitigates the many unhealthy eating behaviours that go along with it. An athletic viewpoint helps one focus more on the nutrition of food and less on calories. This is a much healthier relationship with both food and your body and will serve you very well for years to come.

Now let's move on to another concept you need to know as you are still defining an athlete—the energy system being used during the sport of your choice.

3

HOW THE BODY USES FUEL DURING EXERCISE

Trust me, energy does not come from will power alone. We all have a fancy system in our bodies which manages our energy needs as and when required. Scientifically speaking, this is called the 'Metabolic Energy System' and it refers to how your body is going to produce the muscular energy needed to perform a given sport. As each sport is slightly different in the way it's played, different sports place different demands on the body.

Nutritionally, energy is derived from the food that we eat and the food that we have stored. Let's understand this better: carbohydrates you consume get stored as glycogen in the liver and muscles, protein is broken down into amino acids and get stored in the muscles, and fats get stored in the adipose tissue. When energy demands increase, glycogen, amino acids and fats get converted into glucose to provide energy.

The energy requirements vary and the source of energy differs from sport to sport. For instance, running 5 kilometres requires a different type of effort (mostly aerobic effort, which means that more oxygen is required to perform the activity and hence, it utilizes more fat as a source of energy) as compared to sprinting for 100 metres (which is anaerobic energy, and not dependent on oxygen supply using more of the circulating glucose and stored glycogen as energy for the first few seconds). These are two classic examples of how different energy systems are being utilized in the body.

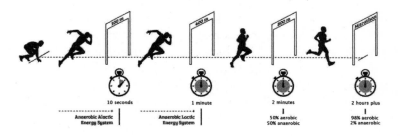

The three energy systems that the human body can rely on during physical activity are:

- The race car or the anaerobic ATP–CP system
- The sports car or the glycolytic system
- The economy car or the aerobic system

Let me explain each of these systems and then provide a table of comparison at the end.

The Race Car or the Anaerobic ATP–CP System

The ATP–CP system uses a source of fuel called adenosine triphosphate (ATP), which is direct energy and is utilized for very brief but highly intense bouts of exercise—just like a speeding race car.

This energy system is used for activities like:

1. Sprinting 100 metres
2. Picking up heavy weights and performing three repetitions
3. Throwing a javelin across a field

These sports require very powerful bursts of energy and hence, this energy system is quickest to fatigue and die out rapidly. Your body has enough existing ATP energy stores in the muscle to last approximately two seconds of intense exercise. Beyond that point, it gets exhausted. It needs something to continue yielding ATP, which comes from creatine phosphate (CP). CP gets synthesized in the muscles to allow you to exercise a little longer and delay the onset of fatigue.

Hence, your ability to keep exercising will be directly linked to how much CP you have stored in your muscles. This is also one major reason why many athletes take creatine supplements, which we will discuss in detail a little later.

Remember that this energy system is much like a race car—it will enable the most intense possible form of exercise for a very short time span. This system will typically allow for up to 8–10 seconds of maximum effort. Once you continue to exercise beyond this time frame, the glycolytic system begins to take over.

The Sports Car or the Glycolytic System

The next system that comes into play is the glycolytic system, which is sometimes also referred to as the lactic acid system. This system relies on glucose as a fuel source, which is what the body turns to once the CP levels have been depleted. Because it takes longer for glucose to convert into a useable form of energy (ATP), you cannot perform an activity at a very high intensity for a long period of time, which is the difference between a race car and a sports car. Fuel production simply wouldn't match fuel utilization. However, at a lower intensity level less fuel is used so that the body can sustain a level of production. Confused? What I mean is that high-intensity activity can be performed only for a short duration due to the demand and supply energy issues of the body.

In addition to the glucose present in the bloodstream, the body can also use stored muscle glycogen to produce energy. This is why eating carbohydrates immediately after training to replenish muscle glycogen levels is so critical to success. After training, your muscles will soak up the glucose from the carbohydrates you eat, storing them in the muscle for use during your next workout. This sports car system will carry you through intense exercise for up to around the two-minute mark, at which point 'the burn' occurs and you will just have to stop.

Ever experienced a burn? Here's a challenge for you. Stand upright, put your hands by your head, your feet shoulder-width apart and start squatting. Do as many squats as you can in a three-minute period. Did you feel the burn? Before those three minutes were up, you would have felt like your quads are on fire and it's all because of the excess lactic acid built up in your system.

If you choose to continue your workout beyond this point, you will gradually enter the next system where the intensity needs to be significantly reduced as the duration of the exercise becomes longer.

The Economy Car or the Aerobic System

Once the glycolytic system is nearing exhaustion, the aerobic system steps into play. Both the ATP–CP and glycolytic systems do not use oxygen and are anaerobic forms of exercise.

Aerobic exercise is just the opposite and occurs using oxygen, which is what helps you sustain it for long periods of time. With the increase in oxygen coming in, your blood will not maintain high acidity levels (as observed in the glycolytic system) and as such, that intense burning and high level of fatigue will not kick in which otherwise forces you to stop.

Like an economy car, the aerobic system is one that can be sustained for hours at a time (with proper training and nutrition obviously), but will require that the overall exercise intensity is lower. This energy system occurs in any activity lasting longer than two minutes, and it encompasses all types of endurance-related activities.

An important point to note about the aerobic system pathway is that it can also use fatty acids as a fuel source. While the glycolytic system can only use glucose as a fuel source (since fat cannot be broken down fast enough to provide energy), the aerobic system runs just as well using fat for fuel.

So for instance, eating carbohydrates before a thirty-minute jog will not be nearly as essential as eating them before doing ten sprints of thirty seconds each. Basically, you can still benefit and see better performance from eating carbohydrates before a moderate-intensity workout, but they just aren't essential.

The bottom line is that the longer the duration of the activity and the more the oxygen used, the better is the fat supply for energy. Although bear in mind that fats need to be combined with carbohydrates in order to last longer through the workout. However, the shorter the duration of the activity, the higher the dependence on carbohydrates for energy without any fat requirement.

As you think of these energy systems, picture someone who is sprinting at the start, slowing down slightly as the sprint continues and then eventually moving into a light jog as they continue the workout. They would be moving through all three systems, starting with the ATP–CP pathway, then moving into the glycolytic pathway, and finishing up in the aerobic pathway.

However, if enough rest is taken between rounds of training, you can remain in the ATP–CP pathway without reaching the glycolytic or aerobic pathway. This is because sufficient periods of rest allow the regeneration of ATP–CP for the next round of training.

The table below summarizes these energy systems:

	ATP–CP System	Glycolytic System	Aerobic System
Duration of Exercise	0–10 seconds	10 seconds–2 minutes	2+ minutes
Intensity of Exercise	Very intense	Intense	Low intensity
Fuel Utilized	ATP ATP–CP	Blood Glucose Glycogen (from the muscle and liver)	Blood Glucose Glycogen (from muscle and liver) Fatty Acids (from the blood or fat tissue)
Example of Relevant Sports	Athletics	Football	Long-distance running

Now that we've gone over the classification of the different body types and energy systems, let's understand the classification of sports.

4

UNDERSTANDING SPORTS

Just as there are many different body types out there, there are also many different types of sports. As a result, you will be able to find a sport that—based on your body type—you can easily excel at. Each type of sport requires a different overall style of training and nutrition, so let's go through the broad classification of sports:

- Endurance sports
- Power sports that use energy immediately
- Power sports that use energy intermittently
- Power and endurance sports

It's not as complicated as it sounds. Let's go through each one of them a little more closely.

Endurance Sports

Endurance sports are those sports that have you doing some form of exercise or activity for a long duration of time. As you have probably guessed, endurance sports use the aerobic energy system. Examples of endurance sports include walking, marathons (or other long-distance running), long-distance swimming, long-distance cycling, long-distance rowing, triathlon events and golf. These sports are typically played using moderate intensity exercise, which allow them to be carried out for a longer duration of time.

Athletes training for these sports will naturally train almost exclusively using the aerobic energy systems. However, they may do a few training sessions in the glycolytic range such as sprint-swim sessions or High-Intensity Interval Training (HIIT) workouts. By doing so, their body adapts to working at a higher intensity level. Their body will delay lactic acid formation, which otherwise causes burns and makes them give up the workout.

Endurance athletes are typically those who have the ectomorph body type, or who have trained their body and it has taken on properties of this body type. Ever noticed a professional marathoner? They rarely have high volumes of muscle on them because muscle mass weighs them down when trying to run those long distances.

Finally, the nutrition plan of these athletes will typically favour both carbohydrates and dietary fat as fuel sources because at this intensity level, they are able to effectively use both to power through their activity.

Power Sports That Use Energy Immediately

The next type of sports we need to consider are sports that utilize an immediate energy source to generate power. These are sports in which there is a sudden burst of energy followed by a lengthy rest period. As you might have guessed, these sports rely almost exclusively on the ATP–CP system. Examples of these sports include weightlifting and bodybuilding, track-and-field sports and sprints in cycling, swimming and running.

These sports utilize very intense activity in an all-out fashion. For instance, if you take weightlifting, an athlete will lift a very heavy amount of weight, performing typically somewhere between 3–12 repetitions, lasting anywhere from ten to forty-five seconds.

The weight the individual lifts directly correlates with the total number of repetitions being performed. If they aim to lift the maximum amount of weight possible, they'll work in the 3–5 repetitions range, thus using ATP–CP energy. These types of sports require specific downtime for rest and recovery to sustain future rounds of exercise at a near equal level of intensity. Athletes training for these sports are best served through training in anaerobic ATP–CP and glycolytic energy systems.

Correspondingly their nutrition protocol will need to be rich in carbohydrates since they are unable to rely on fatty acids as a fuel source. The total intake of carbohydrates will depend on how many total repetitions they are performing. For instance, if an athlete just does three lifts in a given session, they aren't going to need as many carbohydrates as an athlete who does ten or more. In many cases, these athletes will also be the ones using creatine phosphate supplements. These supplements will help increase their overall creatine stores, making it easier for them to sustain high-intensity muscle contraction.

These athletes will typically have the mesomorph body type but they may also be endomorphs who have been training hard to lose excess body fat and build more lean muscle mass.

Power Sports That Use Energy Intermittently

The next category of sports is similar to the previous one, except this time athletes are not focused on just one all-out effort and rather, the effort is intermittent. For instance, with weightlifting the athlete will perform one round of activity with maximum power. But with a sport like tennis, the athlete has to perform multiple rounds using maximum force, requiring powerful hits along with sprints, followed by a rest period in-between. Have you played or seen long rallies on a tennis court? Play usually consists of powerful hits, sprinting line to line and taking a breather after making a point—and then doing this over and over again.

For such sports, training involves doing more repetitions. For example, they might do 20-metre repeats. Here, the athlete would run for 20 metres, rest for a few minutes, start up and run for another 20 metres again and so forth.

Classic examples of these types of sports are badminton, table tennis, squash and kabaddi. These athletes need training to produce a high degree of force and sustain it so that they can keep on playing throughout the entire round. If they fatigue after that first burst of activity, they won't be able to sustain the performance necessary to see success.

These sports also rely heavily on glucose and stored carbohydrates due to the higher number of intense rounds of exercise, so a higher carbohydrate diet is often required. Additionally, ATP–CP is extremely important to generate, recycle and regenerate instant power intermittently while playing such sports.

Any body type, with the right sort of training, can typically perform these sports. However, it's usually the ectomorphs and endomorphs that lean towards these activities.

Power and Endurance Sports

Finally, the last type of sports are those that are a combination of power and endurance. In these sports, the individual has to work hard during certain portions of play and then will back off and work at a much lower intensity level during other portions of play.

Some examples of these power and endurance sports include football as well as cricket. With cricket, both the batsman and the bowler need to have power for their intermittent bursts of energy as well as endurance to last them through the entire game. Despite using the same energy systems, however, they need to train differently because the way they use these systems will vary based on the position they play.

For instance, a batsman is likely to be performing far more endurance activity as he runs around the pitch (unless he decides to only score boundaries). Therefore, his training also needs to be structured differently.

Those athletes who use both power as well as endurance skills throughout their sport will need to spend time doing sprint-like training along with cardiovascular endurance conditioning. Because there is an endurance component to these sports, athletes will need to consume a mix of carbohydrates and fats as fuel so that they have both glucose as well as fatty acids to utilize. This will also help them sustain the high level of power needed for the sport. Again, either of the three body types can excel at these sports with the proper level of training and nutrition.

So there you have a closer look at the main four types of sport classifications. Any sport you come across can be grouped into one of these four categories. Do keep in mind that the position you play in a particular sport could influence which classification it falls into. As a result, it's very important to consider your role in the gym when devising both training and nutritional protocols to follow.

Now that you have a much better idea of what your body type is and the types of sports you can participate in, let's talk about the basics of good nutrition.

PART II

BUILDING AN ATHLETIC LIFESTYLE

If you truly want to obtain an athletic body, a few training sessions here and there won't do the trick. Well, you don't need to change your entire life and live like an athlete, although it's an amazing feeling. But changing your approach and getting more focused on your physical and psychological well-being will help you optimize your performance and bring you a sense of unmatched achievement.

In this section, we'll look at how to go about making the decision to lead an athletic lifestyle. We'll also look at what changes it will entail in your daily life.

5

DECIDING TO BECOME AN ATHLETE

Before delving into the workouts or nutrition information, ask yourself the following questions: Do you have what it takes to achieve an athletic body? Are you prepared to sustain new athletic activities? Can you embrace athleticism as your new way of life? Although you don't need to win a race or a game, are you ready to take up a sport that will challenge you?

Let's go over some of the key things to consider as you are making this decision.

Identifying Your Motivations

Start by looking at why you want to become like an athlete. What's driving this decision?

- Were you an athlete during your childhood and now want to recapture that spirit?
- Perhaps you've never been an athlete but it's something that you've always wanted to do?

- Are you someone who simply wants a change in your life—something new to strive for and work towards in order to improve yourself?
- Is it that you want to achieve a toned, athletic and fit body?

Whatever the case may be, examine your reasons carefully. The first thing you must make sure is that the reason you are doing this is for *you*. Don't take up anything because you are giving into peer pressure. If deep inside you don't really want to take up athleticism, find something else to do with your time and energy because you simply won't sustain the lifestyle changes necessary to make the athletic lifestyle possible.

Firstly, becoming an athlete doesn't need to completely change your life; it just needs to change your approach. Rather than just eating whatever comes your way, you have a different priority: superior performance. You need to pay a much higher level of attention to what you eat and how you go about your routine.

The second thing that you need to remember is that you should have a long-term focus; this cannot be something you are doing on a whim. It's not something that you plan to work towards for a few months and then give up on but rather, being an athlete is something you are making a part of a new lifestyle that works for you. Remember, you get to choose just how involved you become, so choose something that you can comfortably maintain. If you can't exercise for five hours per week, don't start with a plan that calls for that much exercise time. Instead, find a realistic fitness plan that has you exercising three days per week if that's more reasonable. You can still see excellent benefits and train like an athlete with this level of commitment as well. It's all about what works for you.

If the underlying reasons for your becoming an athlete are in tune with these requirements, then you are on the path to success.

Finding Your Inner Drive and Motivation

Next, you need to figure out where your inner drive and motivation come from. Are you looking to gain acceptance from others? Perhaps you want to boost your own self-confidence and love the feeling of others looking up to you? Or maybe your motivation is related to health. You want to live a long and healthy life and be very active as you grow older. My personal motivation was my father's fitness. His strength and vigour as a squash player was so great that he could leave sixteen-year-olds gasping for breath. At some point I felt that if my father could be in peak physical condition at forty-five, anyone could be an athlete.

Others may be more motivated by the feeling of success. They know that when they work hard towards something and then realize success, that feeling of accomplishment is like no other and this pushes them forward—like a marathon runner competing for their personal best or a woman post pregnancy working hard to get back to her own pre-pregnancy weight. Sometimes people can't do this alone. They need a push to make them get to their goal: being accountable to someone in their life, speaking to a successful person who has achieved their body weight target, being answerable to someone they know they can't lie to or even just maintaining a food diary. Recognizing your sources of drive and motivation will be important because you can then focus on these sources as you get going, using them to fuel you through the hard times.

If you don't really know what motivates you, it's a good idea to stop and do some good self-reflection to pinpoint this before you attempt to move forward. It really will make a big difference to your willingness to stick with your regime even when you are completely unmotivated.

Assessing Your Perseverance

You should also take stock of your own individual perseverance. Think back to other times you've set goals for yourself in life and this doesn't have to be related to fitness or sports—it could be any goal you've set. Did you stick it out? When the task became challenging or when you were completely unmotivated, did you quit and throw in the towel? Or did you do whatever it took to get the job done? If you are someone who hasn't been very persistent in your life, you'll need to figure out a way to change this so that moving forward, you can stick to your goals no matter what comes your way.

Because if there's one thing that all athletes have in common, it's that they're persistent. Look at Rahul Dravid and you will understand what persistence means. There is an evident passion he brings out in his sport. His performance always has been consistent and the zeal with which he practises is the same even after years of being at the top of his game. You will face some expected set backs such as muscle soreness, injuries, hunger and exhaustion at different times. But if you don't know how to overcome them and keep on putting one foot in front of the other, you'll never reach your goals.

So take some time now and figure out why you tend to easily lose motivation if you do and what you can do to put a stop to that. Going in prepared to tackle the goal of becoming like an athlete and adopting an athletic lifestyle is going to position you for success. You want to dive right in—fully prepared, focused and ready.

Now let's talk about what your daily schedule is going to be like when you take on the athletic lifestyle.

6

DEVELOPING THE ATHLETIC LIFESTYLE

After making the decision to adopt an athletic lifestyle, you now need to consider what changes you will need to make to your daily schedule. While planning your nutrition and getting started with workout sessions are obviously the very first things you need to do, those are not the only things to be looking out for.

Let's go over a few other aspects you should consider when moving forward.

Early Mornings

There will likely come a time when you need to start training first thing in the morning. Truly dedicated athletes are up before everyone else, hitting the gym, court, pool or track, wherever they happen to be training. But don't let that scare you. You may not be a morning person today, but you will realize with time that you are performing best when the sun is rising. While you will certainly do your share of evening sessions as well, the morning is a primary time to train as you're not tired from the day and nothing will squeeze that workout out of your schedule (other than your hitting the snooze button perhaps!).

You'll eventually adjust to waking up earlier than you likely have in the past and will be ready to exercise at these hours. In case you strongly differ with this point of view, and there is no way in this universe you could be a morning person, don't worry. Evening workouts can help you achieve your athletic body as well.

Meal Preparation Time

The next difference you'll notice is the amount of time you spend cooking and preparing meals.

You need to feed your body properly, so you can't rely on fast food and convenience store food as you may be used to. You need to always eat carefully prepared meals or snacks (which we will discuss later in the book) so that you can fuel your body correctly and sustain your energy for training purposes. This means devoting time each week to meal preparation. Most athletes are best served by dedicating one or two days a week in which they spend an hour or two preparing their meal schedules for the coming week or even fortnight. This way you'll never have a reason to order a buttered, grilled sandwich or buy an unnecessary packet of creamy biscuits.

You'll also likely be spending more time eating than you did before. As your energy demands go up, so must your food intake. You'll likely be eating four to six meals per day (maybe even more if you are very active), so you'll need to make additional time to eat.

Often, this particular adjustment tends to be the hardest one for most people as they move into an athletic lifestyle. However, when you see the difference that proper nutrition makes on how you feel and perform, you won't think twice about doing it. You'll simply know that it needs to be done.

Sleep Schedule Adjustments

Another big part of leading an athletic lifestyle is tending to your sleep. Athletes will need to sleep longer, on average, than non-athletic individuals as this is the time when their body goes into deep-tissue repair.

If you aren't sleeping enough, you'll be more prone to suffering from slow and sluggish recovery rates and poor performance, and you might also find that your risk of injury goes up as well. All in all, you'll find a big lifestyle adjustment based around sleep. You should aim for at least eight hours of sleep per night, if not nine. Given the fact that you will be waking up earlier for those early morning sessions, this means going to bed earlier.

You may have joined your friends on a Saturday night and stayed out until 1 a.m. However, if you now have a Sunday morning training session at 7 a.m., you'll have to start convincing your friends to get the party going on a Friday night. And good friends will be happy to adjust to your new life goals.

Being able to make this commitment to your sport of choice is important to success. Always remember that you get what you put in. If you don't want to get the sleep necessary for you, no one will force you to, but you simply won't see the results that you're hoping to otherwise.

Recovery Activities

Finally, the last of the key lifestyle changes you'll need to get into place is a dedication to recovery activities. You'll need to tend to your body after each training session, ensuring that you are doing what it takes to recover from the workout as fast as possible so that you can train again.

These recovery activities might involve spending more time doing stretching and flexibility work, icing nagging injuries, taking hot baths to promote circulation and recovery, foam rolling (a pressure technique used to open knots in tense and tight muscles with the help of a foam roller, a ball or the hands), as well as going for massages or treatments supervised by a physiotherapist.

All of these recovery activities are going to add time to your daily routine that you need to be ready to cope with. If you aren't, you'll soon find that you aren't bouncing back as quickly as you had hoped from your workout sessions and that it's getting harder and harder to keep up with the training demands your programme is placing on you.

So these are the main changes that you can expect to see as you embark on an athletic lifestyle. You need to be fully prepared to welcome these changes and embrace them for all the good that they are going to do for you.

PART III

NUTRITION 101

This section is not only a beginner's guide for understanding the various aspects of nutrition but it will also help you differentiate between run-of-the-mill, calorie-deficit, weight-loss diets and healthy, sustainable and nutritious meal plans. And this can be achieved by learning and incorporating concepts of sports nutrition into your fitness regime. So let's build our awareness about sports nutrition.

7

IT'S SPORTS NUTRITION, NOT A DIET

What comes to your mind when you hear the phrase 'sports nutrition'? You might immediately think of sports supplements along with sports drinks. Or you might think of a high-calorie diet full of carbohydrates.

The true definition of sports nutrition is focusing on eating right to better your athletic performance. What can you do, nutrition-wise, to ensure that you are putting forth optimal performance?

When you look at most diets, they have one goal: decrease body weight.

It isn't even that they want to decrease body fat so much. In many cases, it's simply body weight they want off. Most diets do this by cutting out calories, often eliminating entire food groups from the diet.

As soon as you are eliminating an entire food group, you know that you'll be at risk for putting your body at a nutritional deficiency. Depending on the nutrient in question, a deficiency can have a number of side effects including a weakened immune system, a lower level of new cell development, decreased energy levels and an increased risk for many diseases and health conditions.

Most diet plans also leave individuals with an unhealthy relationship with food. Some nutritionists prescribe such restrictive plans that after the diet is over, the individual almost feels scared to eat more food again out of fear of weight gain. Some individuals, because they have been so restricted for so long, begin to pig out with pure vengeance. And let's not forget the unsustainable plans of using special diet products like meal replacements or shakes which don't teach people how to eat healthy at all.

In contrast, a proper sports nutrition plan can help you:

- Build and sustain more energy during training sessions, games, races and events.
- Recover faster from any exercise or training.
- Build lean muscle mass.
- Increase your overall speed and power, therefore increasing your performance levels.
- Help manage your body fat levels.
- Keep your immune system strong so that you can handle the stressors of daily training.
- Help optimize your overall health and reduce the risk of a number of different diseases.

While you may think that sports nutrition only applies to high-level athletes, it is a concept that anyone can follow and benefit from even if you are a weekend warrior who only participates in exercise or sports on your days off.

Sports nutrition also looks at food intake as a whole. Rather than focusing only on specific elements, such as calories for instance, which is what many conventional diet plans do, sports nutrition looks at calories in context of the activity along with basic nutrients, hydration and much else.

Basically, you look at the big picture. This helps ensure that no part of your nutrition plan is overlooked and that you maximize everything you can do to achieve your healthiest body ever.

When thinking about sports nutrition and the fact that it focuses on improving performance, you might jump to the conclusion that 'performance' refers to anything related to how well you can exercise. But you should consider performance on the whole too. Performance can also be how well your heart is able to pump blood throughout your body all day long. Or it could be how strong your bones are so that you can complete day-to-day activities without suffering from stress fractures.

Thus, performance is your being able to live optimally because of a body that's strong, fit and healthy. While there's no denying that the main focus of sports nutrition is performance in sports, remember that if you aren't performing well in daily life, you'll never perform well at sports. The benefits of sports nutrition begin at this fundamental level.

Sadly, many people in today's society, due to years of unhealthy eating, aren't performing optimally in their daily lives. And hence, when they start on a sports performance plan the first benefits will be apparent in their daily lives. Then, once they feel better in a general sense, they will begin to see great improvements on the athletic front because the individual will finally be able to put forth the energy they need to participate in their chosen sport.

Broadly speaking, a sports nutrition plan is different from a conventional diet plan.

One key point to remember about sports nutrition is that while certain supplements are definitely used and encouraged, the foundation of the nutrition plan will be around whole foods. This approach will teach you how to structure meals that will not only promote optimal health, but also keep your body functioning at its best.

Hopefully you now have a better idea about what sports nutrition is and why it's simply the best way to tend to your food intake as opposed to any other conventional diet plan. Now let's move forward and talk about the two key elements of nutrition that you need to know: macronutrients and micronutrients.

8

MACRONUTRIENTS

Whenever you put any food into your mouth, it is going to contain nutrients, which give food its definition. For instance, bread is classified as 'carbs' because it is rich in carbohydrates, which is a macronutrient.

The basic nutrients of food are macronutrients and if the food is of a healthy variety, it will also contain micronutrients. Macronutrients are called 'macro' because they are consumed in large quantities as part of your daily food intake and are calculated using large units. Macronutrients consist of proteins, carbohydrates, dietary fats and water—all of which I'm sure you have heard of before. Each of these macronutrients plays a different role in the body and will impact you in various ways.

A proper sports nutrition plan will have you eating a balanced level of each of these nutrients. Except water, macronutrients provide energy and contain calories, which is the unit of energy that the body uses for fuel.

The approximate calories in the various macronutrients are as follows:

	Protein	Carbohydrates	Dietary Fat	Water
Calories	4 calories/ gram	4 calories/gram	9 calories/ gram	0 calories/ gram

As you can see, fat is more than twice as calorie dense as protein or carbohydrates, meaning you don't need to take in all that much food for your energy intake to increase dramatically. Water, on the other hand, is calorie free.

For athletes aiming to be at a certain body weight and body composition level, paying attention to their overall calorie intake will be critical to success. Eating healthy food isn't enough—they need to eat the *right amount* of healthy food in order to get the weight-control results they're looking for.

Two other important foods that generate calories are alcohol and insoluble fibre. Firstly, alcohol provides calories, but these are not considered nutritional for the body as they supply no micronutrients (which we'll be getting to shortly).

Alcohol contains 7 calories per gram but it doesn't provide any energy. So while it's not as calorie dense as dietary fat, it's more calorie dense than both proteins and carbohydrates. This is one reason why consuming alcohol regularly can set you up for fat gain. Apart from being full of useless calories, it also weakens your resolve and willpower to eat healthy foods. Try and remember what you ate at 3 a.m. after a full night of drinking. My guess is that even if you do remember, it wouldn't have been the healthiest choice. Alcohol also hampers protein synthesis, which means that any post-exercise recovery in your body will progress much more slowly than if you hadn't had the alcohol in the first place.

The other important factor is insoluble dietary fibre. While fibre is considered to be a form of carbohydrates, insoluble fibre does not get fully digested in the body and is, therefore, passed out of the system. Dietary fibre is an incredibly important component of your diet and we will talk about it in detail a little later in the book.

As far as calories go, however, 1 gram of dietary fibre contains only 2 calories and this is half of what non-dietary fibre carbohydrates will provide you (at 4 calories per gram). This is one of the reasons that diets rich in dietary fibre can help with weight control. Hence, it is essential that you take these two factors into consideration while thinking about the calories that each macronutrient provides.

Now, in addition to the energy-providing macronutrients, you also have micronutrients which do not contain any energy, but they serve a wide array of important functions in the body. They are found within macronutrients and are classified as vitamins and minerals. They are also called micronutrients because, in comparison to macronutrients, you take smaller doses of these each day.

These micronutrients, which consist of vitamins (both water-soluble and fat-soluble) as well as minerals, are found in nutrient-dense foods and will help to optimize your overall body functions. These are the nutrients that you tend to run the greatest risk of being deficient in if you are not eating healthy foods. For example, if you eat a diet that's high in processed foods and sugar, both of which contain very few micronutrients, over time, you'll have a deficiency in certain vitamins and minerals.

Contrast this with someone who eats a diet rich in fresh fruits and vegetables, lean proteins, wholesome grains, and healthy fats from oils, nuts and seeds, and you will see a completely different story. This is why it's important that you not only pay attention to *how* much food you are eating, but the *type* of food you are consuming as well. When you get the right amount and the perfect variety in, you will function optimally.

Let's now break it down further and delve into each of the macronutrients and micronutrients.

Macronutrients: Protein

The very first macronutrient we will discuss is protein. When most people hear the word 'protein', they tend to immediately think, 'Ah! This is what muscles are made out of.' While it's true that muscles consist of protein, this is definitely not the only role that protein plays in the human body.

Protein is often considered to be the most essential macronutrient that must be consumed daily because you simply would not be able to survive very long without it. About 20 per cent of your body is made up of protein, which should tell you just how important it is.

Protein, which is made up of individual amino acids, provides the building blocks that your body uses to make new cells. In addition, protein is also responsible for giving cells structure, transporting and storing other nutrients in the body, and ensuring that the organs and glands of the body are functioning normally.

Protein is also what makes up your tendons, bones, arteries and skin and is used to repair all of these tissues whenever any damage occurs. Finally, the amino acids from protein are also used to generate hormones and neurotransmitters, which serve as chemical messengers that move throughout the body. They serve to regulate the body through the many actions of your organs, glands and brain. Essentially, neurotransmitters are what your brain and body use to talk to each other. So as you can see, protein plays a very large role in the human body other than just building bulk.

For athletes, protein requirements are much higher when compared to those who aren't exercising regularly because there will be a higher breakdown of their muscle tissues, thanks to all the exercise.

Yes! You read that right. Exercise breaks down muscle tissue before it actually begins rebuilding it. As muscle tissue breaks down, more protein will be needed to build it back up again, which in turn is what causes you to become stronger than you were before.

Take an individual who lifts weights for example. They go to the gym and begin lifting weights that are challenging for their body, to the point of fatigue. As they do this, they create tiny micro-tears in their muscle fibre. The body constantly wants to maintain a state of balance, meaning that it wants to avoid suffering from this breakdown in the future. The body is motivated enough to make sure that the next time it has to face that same activity again—in this case lifting the weights—it can do so without the challenge.

So as time passes, when you leave the gym, your body gets to work immediately, repairing those tears and ensuring the muscles are capable of handling that amount of weight next time. The result is that you have just made progress. This is an ongoing process that will occur throughout your athletic training as you continue to become stronger and better.

Protein, which is made up of different amino acids, can be classified into essential amino acids and non-essential amino acids. The essential amino acids are those that you absolutely must obtain through food sources because your body is unable to make them on its own. Because your body is unable to store these amino acids in bodily tissue, you must get them from your diet in order to maintain optimal functioning capacity. The other amino acids are non-essential and conditional. Don't let this allow you to think that you don't need these amino acids. You do need them, but your body can produce them on its own so they aren't essential as part of your diet plan.

There is a third kind of amino acids as well. Conditional amino acids are those that your body may not be able to produce properly during certain times in your life, such as when you are under high amounts of stress or recovering from a major health problem like surgery. In such times, these acids are considered essential as well. Conditional amino acids include arginine, glutamine, tyrosine, cysteine, glycine and proline.

Sounds confusing? Don't worry, there's no quiz at the end of the book so you don't need to memorize all these funny sounding names!

All you need to know is that there are different types of amino acids or building blocks that combine together in many different ways to form the protein molecules you consume through your diet plan.

If you consume a mixed diet plan with a number of high-quality sources of protein, you shouldn't have any problem meeting your amino-acid needs.

If you want to learn more, this table provides details on particular amino acids and their specific functions in the body:

Amino Acid	Function
Essential Amino Acids	
Leucine	• Provides energy • Reduces muscle protein breakdown • Promotes skin and bone healing
Isoleucine	• Provides energy for muscle cells during exercise • Prevents the breakdown of muscle tissue • Helps form haemoglobin, which transports oxygen throughout the body

Histidine	• Helps absorb ultraviolet light through the skin cells • May help treat those suffering from digestive diseases or rheumatoid arthritis • Is involved in the production of red and white blood cells
Valine	• Moves directly into the blood cells and bypasses the liver • Can assist with energy generation
Lysine	• Ensures protein synthesis takes place at a normal rate • Will help to prevent fatigue in exercising muscle cells when combined with vitamin C • Assists with bone growth through the formation of collagen, cartilage and other connective tissues
Methionine	• Is the precursor of creatine phosphate (used to produce ATP) • Can help reduce blood cholesterol levels • Helps remove toxic waste from the liver • Helps with kidney health
Phenylalanine	• Can help improve learning, memory and alertness • Acts as a mood stabilizer • Can help to manage depression • Helps with the production of collagen • Suppresses the appetite
Threonine	• Can help prevent fatty acid build-up in the liver, preventing fatty liver disease • Is used in the formation of collagen

Tryptophan	• Can exert a calming effect when taken • Helps with the release of the growth hormone in the body
Conditionally Essential Amino Acids	
Arginine	• Helps with the regulation of insulin and glucagon, which are important for managing blood sugar levels • Helps with the production of the growth hormone • May assist in injury rehabilitation through the formation of new collagen • Strengthens the immune system • Helps with healing wounds • Is a precursor to creatine • Breaks down to make nitric oxide
Cysteine	• Can help prevent damage to the body when alcohol is consumed • Stimulates your white blood cells
Glutamine	• Helps you maintain a strong immune system • Can help enhance concentration and memory • Helps in muscle and tissue recovery
Glycine	• Forms a part of the structure of haemoglobin • Can induce a calming effect in the body • Can help to move glycogen out of tissues for use as energy • May lower cravings for sugar

Proline	• Helps form the connective tissue of the body • Helps with the formation of new heart cells • Is used as a muscular energy source • Helps make up collagen
Tyrosine	• Is a precursor to dopamine, which is a feel-good, calming neurotransmitter • Helps with proper thyroid function (which regulates the metabolic rate) • Can help elevate mood
Non-Essential Amino Acids	
Alanine	• Is part of the connective tissue running throughout the body • Helps maintain a strong immune system • Helps in providing muscles and other tissues with energy
Aspartic acid	• Assists with the conversion of carbohydrates into energy in the muscle cells • Helps with the formation of antibodies • Strengthens the immune system • Helps reduce ammonia levels after exercise
Glutamic acid	• Can be used as a source of energy by the body • Is used in the brain's metabolism • Is the precursor for other amino acids

Ornithine	• Helps increase growth hormone secretion • Helps maintain normal liver function • Strengthens the immune system • Promotes healing of body tissues
Serine	• Helps with energy production • Helps with improving memory • Keeps the nervous system functioning optimally • Helps increase immune system strength
Taurine	• Helps with the absorption of fats • May help lower stress levels • Helps with insulin regulation

In addition to the roles noted above, there are a number of other important benefits to eating protein on a regular basis. Let's look at these a little more closely.

Blood Sugar Regulation

The first big benefit of protein is that it has very little influence on blood glucose levels. One of the main ways to sustain stable energy levels throughout the day is to keep your blood sugar levels on an even keel. Those who eat very high carbohydrate diets with little protein or dietary fat will often notice a quick breakdown of those carbohydrates, which then leads to a spike in blood sugar.

While this may cause you to temporarily feel a rush of energy, you hit an energy crash shortly afterwards and will feel worse than you did before. For instance, if you eat a large slice of cake, you might feel like you could jog for hours without tiring but thirty minutes later, you will feel more like taking a snooze on the sofa than exercising.

When protein is consumed with carbohydrates, however, it helps slow the digestion process down, meaning there is no sugar spike. Eating some eggs along with your toast in the morning will help to blunt the blood glucose response. This can then help you maintain a longer lasting source of energy, which is important when you are participating in athletic exercise. Meals with protein tend to 'stick to your ribs', so you'll feel full for hours after eating them. Meals without protein, however, tend to leave you feeling like you're 'running on fumes' shortly after the meal is consumed.

High Thermic Effect of Food

The second key benefit of protein is that it also has a high thermic effect of food (TEF). This means that each and every time you eat protein rich-food, your body is going to expend energy breaking that food down. Some nutrients require far more energy to break down than others, which means that you will actually net fewer total calories when you eat such foods. Protein is an energy-demanding food to break down and you use much of the energy in digesting protein-rich foods, resulting in a higher TEF and eventually achieving fat loss.

The TEF value for protein is around 20–30 per cent while for carbohydrates and fats, it's only about 4 per cent and 2 per cent respectively.

So for every 100 calories of protein that you take in, you can expect to net around 70–80 calories. This is very low when you compare this to carbs, which have you netting around 96 calories and fat, which has you netting 98 calories.

While this may not seem like a very big deal, remember that over time the calories can really add up. Those who want to sustain better body composition and weight control will have an easier time doing so if they make sure their diet has sufficient protein content.

Protein against Lean Muscle Mass Loss

While trying to lose body fat, you will need to lower your total energy intake slightly so that the body can utilize fat as a fuel source. During this time, there will be a greater risk of using the incoming protein as a primary energy source. Should this start to happen, there will be less protein left over for all the important functions of protein such as sustaining your lean muscle mass tissue. This then means that you could begin to see a loss of lean muscle mass, which would cause you to grow weaker and less physically capable as an athlete.

Those who aren't using a reduced calorie intake will typically not have to worry about this as much since they are consuming adequate amounts of carbohydrates and fats to meet their energy needs and saving protein for doing its job. Those who cut back on calories should remember that during this time protein will become more important than it usually is.

The bottom line is that eating a little more protein when you lower your carbohydrates will help make sure that you keep all that hard-earned muscle you've built through exercise!

Greater Satiety

Finally, a major benefit of protein is simply that it helps provide greater satiety. You'll find that after eating a meal rich in protein (along with carbohydrates and/or dietary fats), you feel fuller and more satisfied for longer than if you were to omit protein from the meal. Eating a sandwich at lunch consisting of chicken, bread, vegetables or paneer, chapatti and vegetables will keep you fuller longer than simply eating a bagel with cream cheese or rice and dal would.

Protein helps in regulating your overall food intake and ensures that you feel your best between meals. When you feel ravenous and there's still another two hours until your next meal, you aren't going to be performing optimally as the hunger can serve to be distracting, not to mention lower your energy levels. This feature goes hand in hand with the fact that protein can help stabilize blood glucose levels as well. And hence, these are some important reasons why eating protein in your nutrition plan is a must.

So How Much Protein Do You Need?

Generally speaking, you want to aim for anywhere between 0.8–2 grams per kilogram of body weight for ideal protein intake. Note that the higher side of this range is for active individuals eating a diet that contains a proper amount of calories for optimal performance and daily energy needs. If you are not exercising regularly, you do not need a lot of protein as your body simply won't be experiencing the level of breakdown and rebuilding that comes with vigorous exercise.

While selecting your protein sources, you want to choose those foods that are as natural as possible. Plain chicken breast is a much higher quality protein source than, say, chicken sausages. This is because sausages are processed, and the meat has been altered from its original condition and ingredients (often unhealthy) have been added to it, making it far less nutritionally dense than the plain chicken breast.

Remember that the more you can choose whole foods, the healthier they will always be. If you use this as your guiding principle when it comes to all your food selection, you will do quite well with your nutrition plan.

The table below lists some food sources of protein and the amount of protein a typical serving will contain:

Protein Source	Serving Size	Grams of Protein
Chicken breast	100 grams	31
Turkey breast	100 grams	30
Lean steak	100 grams	30.6
Egg whites	6 whites	26.5
Whole egg	1 large	8
White fish	100 grams	22.8
Low-fat cottage cheese or paneer	½ cup (170 grams)	16
Curd or plain yogurt	¾ cup (100 grams)	16
Milk	1 cup (250 grams)	9
Whey protein powder	1 scoop	20-23
Dals or pulses or sprouts	1 cup (250 grams)	8
Soybeans	½ cup (170 grams)	17.6
Tofu	100 grams	10
Nuts and seeds	½ cup (170 grams)	6

Note: All values provided are for cooked food, unless otherwise indicated.

If you can focus on choosing these foods most often with your meals and snacks, you'll be consuming high-quality amino acids that will do your body good. You should be aiming to include some protein in each meal and snack you consume.

While your snacks may not have as much protein as your meals do, they should still contain at least 8–10 grams to help maintain the sugar levels in the body, increase satiety, improve the thermic effect of the meal and balance out the other nutrients.

Protein will also help you ensure that you have a steady pool of amino acids constantly in your system, providing your muscles with the materials they need for repair and rebuilding. Vegetarians will find themselves turning to the vegetarian foods mentioned towards the end of the table in order to meet their protein requirements. These are all fine foods to eat; just remember that they will also contain higher amounts of carbohydrates and dietary fats, or both.

So now that you have learned about the important macronutrient protein, let's talk about carbohydrates.

Macronutrients: Carbohydrates

How many times have you heard people going 'off-carbs'? Unfortunately, there is much confusion surrounding carbohydrates today. Those who aren't involved in athletic activities very often fear carbohydrates as many have touted them as the reason that so many people are obese. Contradictorily, many athletes, especially endurance athletes like marathoners, tend to have a very large amount of their overall diet focus on carbohydrates to provide them with enough energy in order to delay fatigue.

Neither of these approaches is entirely correct. Athletes will certainly require more carbohydrates than the average, sedentary individual but they need to maintain a balance between carbohydrates and the other two macronutrients. Bear in mind that going to extremes with your diet plan is generally never going to lead to good things. Balance is the key.

If you choose your carbohydrates incorrectly, it can cause you to rapidly gain excess body fat and can put you at risk for a number of diseases. Heart disease and diabetes are two conditions that are currently on the rise and these are usually linked to eating the wrong types of carbohydrates.

But it's not carbohydrates themselves that are the problem; it's the type that we are eating. Popular diets misunderstand and make carbs the bad guy—but the vegetable is also a carb and it's a good carb, fruit is also a carb and a great carb. However, in recent years, as food manufacturing has become so pervasive, more and more items in the grocery store consist of nothing more than processed carbs. These carbohydrates provide very little actual nutritional value because the nutrients—vitamins and minerals—have been stripped from them during the manufacturing process. So right off the start, processed carbohydrates don't do anything positive for the body apart from providing energy.

In terms of the energy these carbs provide, because they are processed, they break down faster than a wholesome carb and spike blood glucose levels quickly. This leads to a rapid boost in energy, which will be followed shortly by a crash.

Let's discuss this process in more depth so that you can see exactly what happens in the body when you consume carbohydrates. Understanding this will help you better classify the different types of carbohydrates.

Carbohydrates in Your Stomach

Whenever you eat carbohydrates, they move through your digestion system where they will eventually be broken down into smaller glucose molecules. Just as protein is made up of amino acids, carbohydrates are made up of glucose. Now, the speed at which those carbohydrates are broken down and glucose is released into the bloodstream will all depend on:

- The type of carbohydrate that you eat (sugar or spinach)

- How much carbohydrate is eaten (a bar of chocolate or a piece of chocolate)
- Whether you are eating carbohydrates with other macronutrients (a vegetable sandwich or an egg sandwich)

When glucose is released into the bloodstream after eating carbohydrates, a hormone called insulin is also released from the pancreas. The role of insulin is to ensure that your blood glucose levels stay within a narrow range that is considered safe for the body. Remember, your body always wants to maintain a state of balance. So if there is something threatening to move it away from this state, it's going to do something to help bring it back.

Insulin will move into your system and will take up the extra glucose, transferring it into storage. Think of insulin as a taxi cab, picking up the glucose molecules (the passengers) and taking them to their home. Their home will either be your muscle tissue,

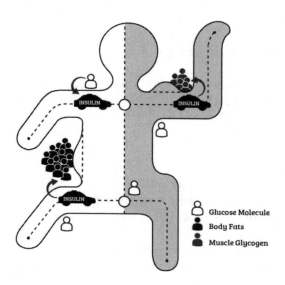

if you have been exercising, where they will then be stored as muscle glycogen, or your body fat stores, if you have not been exercising. Usually, your body fat stores are where they go.

Now, this doesn't mean that every carbohydrate you eat is going to end up in body fat storage. Remember, this applies to only the excess glucose, over and above what you need at that moment.

If your body is releasing glucose very slowly into the bloodstream because of the type of carbohydrate you've eaten, you won't get this large dump of excess glucose and thus, won't have the insulin coming in to push the extra glucose into storage. If you maintain a steady energy level, the insulin secretion in the body is low to non-existent.

Types of Carbohydrates

There are three primary types of carbohydrates you can eat: complex carbohydrates, simple carbohydrates and fibrous carbohydrates. This section covers what you need to know about each of them.

Complex Carbohydrates

Complex carbohydrates, as the name suggests, are complex in nature and will take longer to break down and digest in the body, such as bajra and quinoa. In addition to the type of carbohydrates you eat, you also need to pay attention to how much of these you eat. Let's say you have a have a bottle of sand and you are going to pour it down a funnel in two different ways. In the first instance, you take a quarter cup of sand from the bottle and hold the funnel pointing straight downward. As soon as you pour the sand in, it falls down the funnel and comes out the other end. Essentially, you get one large dump from this quarter cup of sand.

In the second instance, you take one cup of sand from the bottle and are going to pour it down a funnel that is pointed downwards at a forty-five degree angle. Now, the funnel is not pointing straight down and so the sand will pour out more slowly. But at the same time, you have four times as much sand than you had in the first instance. If you had to stand underneath one of these funnels, which would you rather be under? If you answered the one with the quarter cup, you'd be making a smart move. While the sand may come out faster, if it's just a small cup, the amount of sand is not going to be that noticeable. Contrast this to a full cup falling on you and you will quickly see the difference.

So even though the complex carbohydrates may digest more slowly—or fall down the funnel more slowly—if there is a large amount of them in your diet, they are still going to increase blood sugar levels. This is referred to as the GI load.

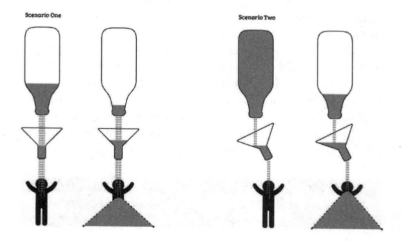

The GI, or the glycaemic index, of a food is the measurement of how quickly the food will break down in the body and release glucose molecules. The glycaemic index is based on a scale of 100, which is the number that pure glucose has. If the food breaks down about as fast as glucose, it would have a GI of somewhere around 90–100. If the food breaks down very slowly, it'll have a GI approximately between 30–40.

While it's important that you focus on low GI, complex carbohydrate foods, if you eat too many of them, will still rank high on the glycaemic load scale (like the sand flowing slowly in the second instance). Just because low GI foods are healthy, they are not to be consumed freely. Proper choices and moderation are the keys to an athletic body.

Another thing to keep in mind with complex carbohydrates is that they are also very energy dense. They will provide you with more energy per serving than some other forms of carbohydrates that we will talk about shortly. So, they should be eaten during periods of the day when you are most active, such as before and after your training sessions and first thing in the morning when you need a good dose of fuel to get your day going.

When choosing your complex carbohydrates, the key to selecting the best varieties is choosing those that are as natural as possible. If a carbohydrate has been altered in any way from its original condition, you know that it isn't as healthy as it once was. The table below shows some of the best choices of complex carbohydrates and an approximate idea of how many grams of carbohydrates they provide:

Carbohydrate Source	Serving Size	Approximate Grams of Carbs
Brown rice	1 cup	44.8
Red rice	1 cup	35
Quinoa	1 cup	39.4
Barley	1 cup	44

Couscous	1 cup	36.5
Oatmeal	½ cup (uncooked)	27.4
Sweet potatoes or yams	1 cup mashed	58.1
All bran cereal	½ cup	34
Dals or pulses	1 cup	40
Millets	1 cup	41.2
Wheat	1 cup	44

All of the carbohydrates listed above are also good sources of dietary fibre, which we'll talk about in more detail as well. For now, remember that fibre helps regulate blood glucose levels even further while also reducing hunger pangs.

Some of these carbohydrate sources, such as dal and pulses, are also good sources of protein. While they won't have as much protein as, say, chicken breast would, they will help contribute more protein to your total daily intake. For those who are struggling to get their needs met, they can be an excellent solution.

Now let's look at the next category of carbohydrates you can consume: simple carbohydrates.

Simple Carbohydrates

Simple carbohydrates, as the name suggests, are simple in nature. Just as complex carbohydrates break down slowly in the body, as you might have guessed, simple carbohydrates break down far more rapidly. These usually are the carbohydrates that you want to avoid the vast majority of the time. By keeping your diet free of simple carbohydrates, you can maintain stable blood glucose levels, keep your energy levels constant and prevent unwanted weight gain.

That said, there is one particular time when simple carbohydrates can actually be helpful. Which is it? Right after your workout or training session.

Immediately after exercise, your muscles are like a sponge, ready to suck up any glucose that comes into your bloodstream to restore muscle glycogen and to help with the rebuilding and repair of muscle tissues. Remember, while the amino acids from protein provide the building blocks to generate muscle tissues, it's the energy from carbohydrates that helps to assemble those building blocks together.

Think of it this way. If you were to build a new addition to your house and you brought just a huge pile of bricks to your to do the job, what would happen? Not much. You'll need workers to actually take those bricks and build the new addition. Think of the workers as the carbohydrates that you eat; they are the ones that make use of the bricks (protein).

Because simple carbohydrates break down quickly, they spike insulin levels that move glucose into tissue storage, which is perfect for this post-workout time. Therefore, the one time of day when you do want to consume some simple carbohydrates is right after you exercise. The rest of the day, they should not be your preferred choice of food.

Now, what foods do we mean when we say simple carbohydrates? In most instances, this refers to any sort of processed carbohydrate that has been altered from its original condition. One very quick and easy technique used to see if a carbohydrate is 'simple' is to look at the ingredient listing on a package. If you see twenty different ingredients all lined up, you know this food is highly processed and will not offer you any health benefits.

One thing to keep in mind as you look at the nutritional label on a food package is that sugar can come in many different forms. The names in the list below are all synonymous for sugar:

- Agave
- Beet sugar
- Blackstrap molasses
- Brown sugar
- Cane sugar
- Confectioner's sugar
- Corn syrup
- Date sugar
- Dextran
- Fructose
- Fruit juice
- Fruit juice concentrate
- Glucose
- Glucose solids
- Golden sugar
- Grape sugar
- High-fructose corn syrup
- Honey
- Icing sugar
- Invert sugar
- Lactose
- Malt syrup
- Maltodextrin
- Maltose
- Maple syrup
- Molasses
- Raw sugar
- Sucrose

While the above list are all ingredients, to give you an idea of what simple sugars look like, some of the most commonly eaten simple carbohydrates include:

- Cakes
- Candy
- Chips
- Chocolate
- Cookies
- Crackers
- Granola bars
- Muffins
- Pastries
- Pretzels
- Soda
- White bread
- White potatoes
- White rice

When selecting foods to eat around your workout, you do want to include some sugar. For instance, having some white rice or white potatoes would be better post your workout, whereas some gummy candies can be munched on during a long-distance cycling event. Use your best judgement on which food suits you the most. However, try and keep things as natural as possible such that you will at least get some nutritional benefits.

Now, another type of simple carbohydrate we need to talk about is fruit.

How Fruit Fits into the Carbohydrate Picture

Fruit is a special type of simple carbohydrate because while it does contain simple carbs in the form of sugar, it also contains a good dose of dietary fibre, which slows the release of glucose into the bloodstream.

In addition, it's important to take note of the type of sugar that fruit contains. Fruit has a mixture of glucose and fructose, which maintain a key distinction. So despite the sugar it contains, fruit will still be ranked relatively low on the GI scale. Fruit ranks higher than most complex carbohydrates on the GI scale, but much lower than, say, soft drinks or cake would be.

Glucose is the only sugar molecule that will spike insulin levels as it is released into the bloodstream. Fructose, on the other hand, doesn't go into the bloodstream but instead into the liver. Your liver can store around 50 grams of fructose per day; fructose will either be stored as liver glycogen here or used for energy (depending on your current physical activity situation). This means fructose will not influence blood glucose levels to the extent pure glucose will, making fruit a safe diet choice.

As most fruit contains around 10–15 grams of total fruit sugars, you can anticipate taking in around 5–8 grams of fructose per serving. This allows you to consume quite a few servings of fruit per day and still stay within the 50 grams of maximum liver glycogen storage.

Keep in mind that if you surpass the fructose limit, your body will quickly convert excess fructose into body fat. This is also why eating non-fruit sources of fructose, such as foods with high-glucose fructose corn syrup, are linked to weight gain. So you do need to be mindful of how much you are eating. It becomes very easy to take in 50 grams of fructose with a few poor food choices, such as drinking soft drinks or other fruit flavoured beverages, putting you at a high risk of gaining body fat.

A final thing about fruit that's important to note is its nutritional density. Fresh fruit contains a wealth of vitamins, minerals and antioxidants, all of which helps keep your body healthy and ward off diseases. From a nutritional standpoint, fruit is one of the best types of foods you can eat and should never be eliminated from a nutrition plan.

As fruit does contain some simple sugars, it's also a great option to eat immediately post workout. High fructose foods (or beverages) are not ideal to consume during athletic exercise. This is because fructose takes some time to be absorbed into the bloodstream, and it won't be available for immediate energy like glucose will. For this reason, save your fructose consumption for before or after your workout instead.

Some fruit does contain more calories and sugar than others. Using this information, you can plan your intake accordingly. The graph below displays the sugar content per one cup serving of some common fruit:

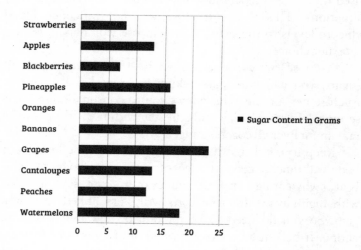

Fibrous Carbohydrates

Now it's time to talk about the last type of carbohydrate: fibrous carbohydrates. These carbohydrates, as the name suggests, contain primarily dietary fibre. This category of carbohydrates encompasses all the fresh vegetables that you can add to your diet plan including foods like broccoli, spinach, collard greens, peppers, mushrooms, cauliflower and cabbage, to name just a few.

When it comes to getting proper nutrition, vegetables simply can't be beaten. Vegetables are nutritional powerhouses, containing a wealth of vitamins, minerals and antioxidants, all of which help you achieve the highest possible health standards. If you have a nutrition plan containing plenty of these foods, you may not need to use a multivitamin supplement like many other people do today.

Another great thing about vegetables (fibrous carbohydrates) is that they are very low in calories. The calorie count is so low in fact that most people will not need to even account for them in their daily food plan. They can simply add them in without worry as they won't amount to much energy overall. This makes vegetables excellent for individuals who are focusing on body composition management. If you are looking to burn up excess body fat while you focus on building lean muscle mass, these foods can certainly help.

This being said, remember that while vegetables are good for body weight management, they are not good for fuelling intense workout sessions. You won't get much energy from a cup of broccoli, and if this is your only source of carbohydrates prior to exercise, it's simply not going to get the job done.

Keeping this in mind, timing your intake of fibrous carbohydrates is very important. They should be added to your diet with most meals for their nutritional value but you should also add complex carbohydrates or fruit around the times when you plan to exercise. This way you get both the nutrition you need from the fibrous carbohydrates along with the energy you need from the complex carbohydrates, which will in turn ensure optimal athletic performance.

The other point to note is that in order for vegetables to maintain their health-boosting properties, they need to be cooked using healthy cooking techniques. If you are deep-frying them, bathing them in sauces and condiments, or adding a large pat of butter at the table, they're no longer going to have the positive impact on your nutrition that you hoped for. As far as possible, try to eat them in as close to their natural state—raw, steamed, sautéed in just a touch of healthy oil, or grilled. This will keep their health benefits intact.

You should also keep in mind that a few vegetables such as peas, carrots, potatoes and corn contain more carbohydrates and sugar or starch. Since they are slightly higher on the GI index, these vegetables will impact blood glucose levels more than other vegetables. It is a wise choice to eat these before or immediately after training. Just remember that you still do need to monitor how much of them you eat to keep your body fat percentage in check.

So there you have a closer look at the three main types of carbohydrates that you can add to your diet plan. Before we move forward and discuss how important these carbohydrates are, let's discuss the concept of dietary fibre.

An Introduction to Dietary Fibre

Dietary fibre is found in many of the carbohydrates that we have already discussed, including complex carbohydrates, fruit and fibrous carbohydrates. There are two types of dietary fibre in the human diet: insoluble dietary fibre and soluble dietary fibre. In order to achieve peak health and nutrition, you want to take in both of these types of fibre.

Let's talk about each one in detail.

Soluble Fibre

Soluble fibre is a fibre type that when digested, attracts water, dissolves, and forms into a gel, which then helps to slow the passage of food through the digestive track. This helps to delay the emptying of the stomach, which creates a greater sense of fullness after eating a meal, helping reduce hunger pangs while you keep your food intake in check.

Because it slows down the digestion process, soluble fibre also helps you manage blood glucose levels better, avoiding those spikes that cause a large amount of insulin to enter your system. This type of fibre may also help to improve insulin sensitivity, which is a term that refers to how well your body's cells respond to insulin when it's secreted. Those who are starting to become insulin resistant (meaning their cells do not respond well at all), will need to release more and more insulin in order for it to do its job, which can, in time, burn out the pancreas and lead to Type 2 diabetes. Because soluble fibre helps to improve your insulin sensitivity, it helps you ward off diabetes. It is also excellent for helping lower bad LDL cholesterol in the blood and reducing plaque formation in the arteries that, in time, can lead to heart attacks.

You'll find soluble fibre in many complex carbohydrates in particular and by choosing the right carbs, you can increase your intake dramatically. Soluble fibre is found in some fresh fruit and vegetables as well and by eating a mixed diet, you can easily increase your intake.

The table below lists some of the best sources of soluble fibre:

Food	Serving Size	Grams of Fibre
Psyllium husk	1 tablespoon	3.5
Oat and/or oat bran	¾ cup	2.2
Black beans	½ cup	2.4
Kidney beans	½ cup	2
Avocado	½ cup	2.1

Brussels sprouts	½ cup	2
Sweet potato	½ cup	1.8
Asparagus	½ cup	1.7
Orange	1 medium-sized piece	1.8
Flaxseed	1 tablespoon	1.1

With regard to athletic training, adding these foods to your diet regularly will help you maintain and stabilize your energy levels throughout the day so that you are able to train harder and perform better. Hence, soluble fibre works as a great pre-workout snack as it helps to release energy slowly and sustainably which helps you work out effectively and delay fatigue.

Insoluble Fibre

The second type of dietary fibre is insoluble fibre. This type of fibre does not dissolve in water but instead, it passes right through the digestive track. It can have a laxative effect when consumed in large doses, so it's important to be careful that you get enough but don't overdo it. You should increase your fibre intake slowly by adding around 4–5 grams every two to three days to let your body adjust and adapt to the increased intake. This will help prevent side effects that would require you to stick close to a bathroom. When you eat the right amount, this type of fibre does a great job of helping keep your bowel movements regular and ensuring that you avoid constipation.

Insoluble fibre will actually speed up the passage of food through your gut, which is actually very healthy and good for your gut. It helps remove toxic waste from the body quickly so it's never just sitting in your system, potentially leading to problems. So while one type of fibre will slow down digestion, the other kind of fibre speeds it up.

This type of fibre will also help to control the acidity (pH) level of the intestines, making sure a healthy pH level that fosters optimal function and performance is maintained. If you eat foods that are very acidic, this can quickly change the overall pH level of the intestines, leading to you feeling unwell over the short-term and increasing your risk for health problems over the long-term. People who constantly have improper pH levels in their intestinal tract may especially be at a greater risk for developing colon cancer.

You can find insoluble fibre in many foods as well, including complex carbohydrates, fruit and vegetables. Here again, eating a balanced, mixed diet is best for increasing your overall intake of insoluble fibre. The table below lists of some of the common sources of insoluble fibre and how much they contain:

Food	Serving Size	Grams of Fibre
Wheat bran	½ cup	11.3
All bran cereal	½ cup	7.2
Kidney beans	½ cup	5.9
Lentils	½ cup	4.6
Wholegrains (bulgur, brown rice, barley, etc.)	½ cup	2-4
Flaxseeds	1 tablespoon	2.2
Lady finger	½ cup	3.1
Peas	½ cup	3
Brussels sprouts	½ cup	1.3

Asparagus	½ cup	1.1
Broccoli	½ cup	1.2
Blackberries	½ cup	0.7
Apricots	4 medium-sized pieces	1.7
Mango	½ cup	1.2

One question that people often ask regarding fibre is whether it actually counts as a carbohydrate in terms of the energy derived. While looking at the calorie content of protein, carbohydrates and fat, both protein and carbohydrates contain 4 calories per gram, while dietary fats contain 9 calories. Fibre in particular has 2 calories per gram. Therefore, by increasing your total daily fibre intake, you actually net fewer calories overall in your diet plan.

Just keep in mind that if you are eating plenty of fibre-rich foods, you may need to eat a little more to ensure that you keep your energy levels up for all the physical activity you plan to do. Dietary fibre is an important nutrient that you must pay attention to if you want to optimize your health, performance, and simply how you feel on a day-to-day basis.

How Much Should You Aim For?

While typical fibre intake in a diet is around 15 grams per day, this is far too low if you are hoping to achieve proper nutrition. Nutrition guidelines are currently set for around 25 grams per day for women under the age of fifty and between 30–38 grams per day for men under the age of fifty. If you are a highly active female and on a particularly high-calorie diet, your fibre intake recommendation will be higher as well.

You don't really need to obsess about how much insoluble versus soluble fibre you take in because as you've likely noted above, both types are found in many of the same high-fibre foods. If you are taking in one type, there's a good chance that you are taking in the other.

Need a little help boosting your fibre intake? Here are some fast and easy tips to help you get started:

- Always eat the skin on fruits (this is where most of the fibre is found).
- Swap the cereals or grains with dals or pulses or sprouts instead as these are a higher fibre food.
- Begin your day with bran cereal or oatmeal.
- Consume raw vegetables as a quick snack on the go (bonus points if you add hummus as a dip—which is also rich in fibre thanks to the chickpeas it contains).
- Prepare stews for dinner, filled with dals or pulses or sprouts.
- Always choose wholegrain products rather than white processed foods (which you should already be doing as part of eliminating simple carbs from your diet plan).
- Go vegetarian once or twice a week. It's the perfect way to boost your intake of fresh fruit and vegetables.
- Add mixed seeds on top of some yogurt to boost the fibre and healthy fat content of your diet.
- Start every meal with a large salad.
- Prepare a stir-fry for dinner, using as many fresh vegetables as possible.

Once you get into the habit of looking for ways to add more fibre into your diet, you'll find that it's relatively easy to get your intake up. Now that we've finished discussing dietary fibre, let's move on to why carbohydrates are important in your athletic nutrition plan.

Why Carbohydrates Are Important

So far we've discussed the fact that there is no need to fear carbohydrates as you develop your nutrition plan. If you choose the right types, you can definitely include them regularly and still be a very healthy individual. In fact, you *must* include them. What many people do not realize is that carbohydrates should not be considered optional in your meal. While you can cut back on them, as in the case of low-carb diet plans, going to extremes is never recommended, especially as far as long-term health is concerned.

There are many reasons why you should be eating carbohydrates, so let's take some time to go through these reasons right now.

Energy

The very first reason to add more carbohydrates to your diet plan is simple: energy. If you've ever done a very low-carb diet before, you've likely felt one thing: extreme fatigue. While things might have been going great for the first week or so, by the time that second week hit, a feeling of tiredness must have hit you like a brick wall. All you probably wanted to do was lie on the sofa and not move.

That's almost always how the situation plays out. Carbohydrates are the primary energy-providing nutrient for the body and if you are not consuming enough, you can be assured you are going to feel it in your daily energy levels. This will then impact your activity levels and soon, your training sessions. If you hope to achieve an athletic body, training is not optional—you need to be doing your sports training dedicatedly. And without the fuel to support that training, you simply aren't going to get very far. It'd be like trying to take your fancy new car out for a drive to another city without putting petrol in the tank first. You won't be able to move an inch.

Think of your body in the same way. Carbohydrates are the highest quality of fuel that you can put into your body, so making sure that you have a steady supply coming in from your diet is a must.

Metabolic Maintenance

The second reason why you should be eating carbohydrates is because they also help you sustain a proper metabolic rate. If you make your carbohydrate intake too low, a hormone in your body known as leptin begins to shift. Think of this hormone like a guard dog against starvation. Leptin's role in the body is to monitor how much total food as well as carbohydrates you're taking in. Whenever food intake becomes too low and starvation may be near, it takes action to push you to eat more. Leptin does this by driving your hunger level through the roof, causing you to become extra tired and making your food cravings so strong that you can't focus on anything but food.

If you hope to feel your best, you want leptin to be regulated at normal levels and eating more carbohydrates can help you do this. Carbohydrates in particular interact with leptin the most, so they must be consumed on a daily basis.

Hunger Control

Speaking of hunger, this also brings us to the next reason to add carbohydrates into your plan. Most people will find that if they are on very low-carb diets, this can really do a number on their hunger as well. As their energy drops, their hunger increases and soon, they just aren't feeling very well. Most people need a balanced meal containing proteins, carbohydrates and dietary fats in order to get the level of satiety they are looking for.

Of course, this is assuming you are choosing the right types of carbohydrates. Not all carbohydrates will have this impact on the body. If you eat simple carbohydrates, they can actually increase your hunger to a level higher than if you hadn't eaten them in the first place.

Proper Brain Function

Now this benefit of eating carbs may sound odd but it's very true. Adding carbohydrates to your diet will help ensure that you maintain proper brain function. If you have ever been on a very low-carb diet before, you may have felt almost like you were in a stupor. Your brain was foggy, you couldn't think straight and your attention level was that of someone with Attention Deficit Hyperactivity Disorder (ADHD). You just couldn't stay focused!

This is the lack of carbohydrates coming into play. Your brain requires glucose on a daily basis in order to function effectively. So when glucose levels are running too low, you see such problems occur. Not only are carbohydrates important for you to think straight and feel your best, they're important for your mood as well. When you eat carbohydrates, your brain releases a particular neurotransmitter called serotonin, which actually makes you feel good.

That's right—when you dig into a slice of cake and suddenly feel happier than before, it's not just because you love cake. There are actually changes taking place in your body that are causing you to feel this way. And it doesn't just happen after you eat cake—it can happen after consuming any type of carbohydrate. This is why on those low-carb diets, you might have felt like you were crankier than normal.

If you omit carbs from your diet plan, you'll be quick to find that those you love and care about start avoiding you. It really takes a toll on your mood. Keeping them in your diet plan, at a reasonable level, helps you sidestep this problem.

Lower Risk Factor for Disease

Carbohydrates also help you lower the risk factor for a number of diseases.

The right carbohydrates may play a role in reducing the risk factor for a wide number of diseases including heart disease, stroke, cancer, depression and diabetes. Interestingly enough, the wrong types of carbohydrates—those simple carbohydrates—will do the opposite. Eat too many of these and you can actually increase the risk factor for these diseases, illustrating how important it is that you choose the right variety of carbs.

Regular Bowel Movements

In the fibre section, we spoke about the fact that insoluble fibre will help you maintain regular bowel movement. This can't be overlooked. There's nothing that will cramp your style more than feeling constipated all the time and yet, for those on low-carb diets, this is very often how the diet plays out.

Without carbohydrates in your plan, you'll be hard-pressed taking in any dietary fibre at all. Pure protein sources (chicken, beef, eggs, etc.) contain no dietary fibre, so you won't get any from there. While you will get small amounts from some sources of healthy fats such as nuts and seeds, it's never going to be enough to help you meet your daily quota. You need carbohydrates—wholegrains, beans and legumes, fruit and vegetables—if you ever hope to meet your daily fibre intake needs.

Lean Muscle Mass Building

Finally, the last reason you should be eating carbohydrates is because they play a key role in helping you generate lean muscle mass. Remember, if you hope to become stronger and more athletic, you will need to focus on adding more lean muscle mass to your frame. This is what will increase your strength, power and overall performance.

But without carbohydrates you will find it very hard to do this. Carbohydrates are what supply the energy for your body to assemble protein (amino acids) into more lean muscle mass tissue and also provide the energy to perform your workouts.

Intense muscular contractions can only use glucose as a fuel source. Thus, you need to be eating carbohydrates before your training sessions. And without training sessions, you simply won't be able to build more lean muscle mass—so you can see how important these really are.

Phew! I hope you realize that there are many reasons why eating carbohydrates as part of your nutrition plan are a must. Don't fear them! Eat them and enjoy every bit of them. Just be sure that you are choosing the right varieties.

Carbohydrate Recommendations

Unlike protein, where there tends to be a very specific amount a person should consume each day, your carbohydrate needs will vary widely depending on your total body weight as well as your activity level and the type of activity you are doing. Someone who is doing a high volume of exercise—say, a marathoner, training for two to three hours every day, is going to need a lot more carbohydrates in their diet than someone who is training for badminton and only playing for an hour a day.

As a baseline level, all individuals should aim for around 2 grams of carbohydrates per kilogram of body weight. This should be sufficient to fuel everyday activities, not including physical training.

The purpose of this much carbohydrate intake is to simply give you energy to shower, prepare your meals, go to the grocery store, and do whatever it is you do at work or school and so forth. Think of carbohydrates as energy for life. Additionally, you'll need to add carbohydrate grams to account for the activity that you are performing. If you are doing an hour of exercise for instance, this may require another 100 grams or so added to your daily total.

You can assume that for every ten minutes of intense exercise, you will be burning around 25–30 grams of carbohydrates. Use this level to estimate how many additional carbohydrates you'll need to fuel the activity you are doing. If you are doing more moderate exercise like a light jog, you will need less, perhaps only 4–5 grams per ten minutes of exercise. One good way to determine if you are eating sufficient carbohydrates is to simply look at how you feel. Do you feel strong? Do you have energy to spare? If so, you are likely eating enough.

If, on the other hand, you feel like you're dragging throughout the day, like every bit of activity you do feels more challenging than it should, then you know that you may need to increase your carb intake. Although lack of energy could be due to many other factors such as low vitamin B12 levels, low haemoglobin, lack of sleep, overtraining and poor recovery etc., it's usually associated with a low intake of carb-rich foods and the complementing vitamins and minerals they include. And remember, you may eat more carbohydrates on some days than others. If you are doing a particularly long and hard training session one day, expect to eat more carbohydrates on that day. You will need it to get through the training as well as to recover quickly from it.

Being able to adjust your meal plan based on the nature of the physical training you are doing is important so that you don't end up gaining unwanted body weight in the process. If you were to eat the same amount of carbohydrates on your rest days as you do on those heavy training days, you will quickly see yourself becoming heavier.

If your goal is to actually build some more lean muscle mass and you are actively doing resistance training, you will want to eat a little more carbohydrates over and above your needs as well. This will provide your body with the extra bit of energy it needs to help form new muscle mass, helping you make the progress you're after. Most athletes will end up taking in around 4–8 grams of carbohydrates per kilogram of body weight, depending on the day and their activity level. You'll need to think about what your weekly training schedule looks like and get a personalized estimation of the carbohydrates you need.

As you can see, carbohydrates aren't the evil nutrient that so many people have come to fear them as today. While it's true that someone who isn't participating in athletic training will need to watch their carbohydrate intake more than someone who is, no individual should ever eliminate carbohydrates entirely from their diet plan. This is one key difference between proper sports nutrition and other carb-free diet plans.

Now let's move forward and talk about the third and final macronutrient we need to discuss here: dietary fat.

Macronutrients: Dietary Fat

Just as some people have come to believe that carbohydrates are an evil nutrient and should be avoided, others tend to believe the same for dietary fat. The thinking here is that by eating dietary fat, one will increase the chances of gaining body fat. People tend to think that when dietary fat goes into the system, it stores directly in the body as fat. However, that is not how things work.

Dietary fat is broken down and digested just as both protein and carbohydrates are, and the only way it will end up as body fat is if you consume too much of it. If you eat the right type of dietary fat in the right amount, it will fuel your body well and help you maintain optimal health. In fact, you need a certain level of dietary fat each day in order to stay alive and function properly.

Just as with carbohydrates, the type of fat you are eating will make all the difference in the results that you see from your diet plan. Let's look at the role that dietary fat has in the body and then discuss the primary types of dietary fat that you need to know about.

Long-term Fuel Storage

The very first reason why you must be eating dietary fat in your diet plan is because it provides a source of long-term fuel storage. Remember when we spoke about the aerobic energy system? Well, the aerobic energy system uses fat as a fuel source and will make good use of any dietary fat you are consuming. If you are participating in endurance-related activities such as marathon running for example, once the carbohydrates in your body are depleted, your body uses fat as a fuel source.

Secondly, while dietary fat won't help much if you are doing intense exercise, they will still fuel the other activities you do during your day, ensuring that all the ATP–CP and glucose in your system is readily available when it is time to exercise.

Blood Sugar Regulation

Another important role of dietary fat is to help with blood sugar regulation. Remember when we discussed how protein and carbohydrates impact blood sugar levels? Dietary fat doesn't cause blood glucose levels to spike at all. In fact, dietary fat can blunt blood sugar levels because it helps to slow the digestion process even further, consequently slowing down the release of glucose into the bloodstream.

Adding just a little dietary fat to your meals, around 5 grams or so per meal, is all that's needed in order to help keep your blood glucose levels in check.

Source of Nutrients

The next reason that dietary fat is a must in any proper nutrition plan is because it will provide you with the key nutrients your body needs to function at an optimal level. Certain vitamins, which we'll talk about in much greater detail shortly, are fat soluble, meaning they will only be absorbed in the body properly when dietary fat is consumed. These vitamins are often found in concentrated doses in fat-rich foods and by eating such foods, you ensure your needs are met. If you are on an ultra low-fat diet, you may start to become deficient in these vitamins, which will then lead to other health problems coming into play.

Those who eat very low-fat diets on a regular basis are simply not going to maintain the same overall health status as those who choose to include this food group in their plan. And it's also true that fat simply tastes good! Fat will help add delicious texture to the foods you eat and increase the flavour too. Most people who force themselves on to a low-fat diet will often fall off the bandwagon simply because the food they are eating isn't appealing enough. Low-fat diets are often referred to as cardboard diets. Fat helps increase the enjoyment of your diet and when you enjoy your diet, you are that much more likely to stick with it.

Hormone Production

Finally, the last reason to include dietary fat in your meal plan is because it plays a key role in the formation of a number of different hormones, primarily the sex hormones. Men, for instance, will rely on dietary fat to some degree for the production of testosterone.

When we look at the key physical performance differences between men and women, it's quite easy to see that men are far stronger than women are, and this is due to the hormone testosterone. So when a man is not getting enough dietary fat, he will find his testosterone level decreasing, which in turn will make him feel weaker and less athletic.

While men do have a large amount of testosterone in their body, women have some too. While in women it's just a fraction of the amount, it will still make a difference to how any woman feels and performs. If she is not getting sufficient dietary fat, she may see a decline in her energy levels as well.

And more importantly, if a woman is not getting sufficient dietary fat, her body may not manufacture enough of the female sex hormones, oestrogen and progesterone, which may then impact her ability to menstruate. Often, female athletes who are dieting intensely and exercising heavily will skip their monthly menstrual cycle, and this is one big reason why. They aren't taking in the energy and dietary fat necessary to keep the menstrual cycle going in their body. If their body is having a hard time supporting itself with the food available, getting pregnant is very difficult as there is an additional life to support as well. This condition is known as athletic amenorrhoea and can occur when an improper diet is followed.

Now that we've discussed the main reasons you need fat in your diet, let's take some time to go over the different types of fats. Not all dietary fats are created equally, so it's imperative that you are eating the right kind of fat to support all around good nutrition.

Types of Dietary Fats

When it comes to fats, there are three main types:

1. Unsaturated fats, comprising monounsaturated fats and polyunsaturated fats
2. Saturated fats
3. Trans fats

Let's go over the details of each of these varieties:

Unsaturated Fats

Unsaturated fats are the good kind of fats in the body. These are the fats that you want include in your meal plan as much as possible, as they will provide a wealth of health benefits along with the other benefits that we noted previously. One way to recognize these fats is that they tend to be liquid at room temperature in pure fat form (oils). There are two primary types of unsaturated fats: monounsaturated fats and polyunsaturated fats.

Monounsaturated Fats

Monounsaturated fats offer a number of health benefits, including:

■ Lowering the risk factors for breast cancer and heart diseases.

- Reducing overall cholesterol levels.
- Helping promote optimal weight loss.
- Decreasing some of the painful symptoms of rheumatoid arthritis.
- Decreasing the level of fat around the abdominal region (when a proper calorie balance is maintained).

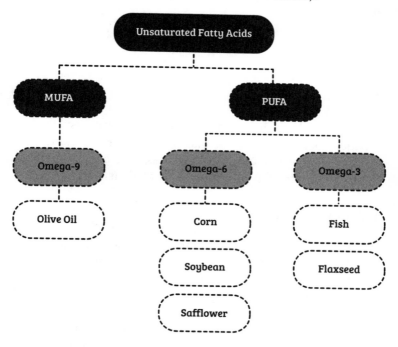

These fats are primarily known for their heart–health boosting benefits. If heart disease runs in your family or it's something that you are concerned about, monounsaturated fats are the kind of fats that want to be consuming. These fats are also a great source of the fat-soluble vitamin E, which has antioxidant effects on the body. This can help reduce the risk factor for cancer.

So where can you find these fats? You'll most often find monounsaturated fats in:

- Olive oil
- Canola oil
- Peanut oil
- Safflower oil
- Sesame oil
- Avocados
- Peanut butter
- Nuts
- Seeds

You should keep in mind that these fats will usually be blended together in a particular food item. For instance, if you eat some peanut butter, you will take in a combination of monounsaturated fats and polyunsaturated fats.

Polyunsaturated Fats

We now come to polyunsaturated fats. These fats are also healthy for the body when you consume the proper foods in the right quantities. Some of the health benefits you'll receive from these fats include:

- Lowering the level of bad cholesterol in the body.
- Reducing the risk factors for stroke and heart disease.
- Helping to maintain and build new body cells.
- Providing antioxidants to decrease the risk factor for cancer.

While these fats do provide many of the same benefits that the monounsaturated fats provide, taking in a combination of both types of fats is important. The primary foods that contain polyunsaturated fats include:

- Sunflower oil
- Corn oil
- Soybean oil
- Flaxseed oil
- Walnuts
- Flaxseeds
- Fish (salmon/rawas, mackerel/bangda, tuna and sardines)
- Canola oil

Moreover, falling under the category of polyunsaturated fats are omega fatty acids. These fatty acids are often referred to as essential fats because your body cannot produce these on its own but rather, it needs to consume them as part of a well-balanced diet plan. There are two primary types of fatty acids: omega-3 and omega-6.

The main thing you need to strive for when it comes to your polyunsaturated fat intake is getting the right balance between these two different types of fatty acids. The problem in most diets today is that we take in far too many omega-6 fatty acids and not enough omega-3 fatty acids, which can lead to many unwanted side effects.

Too many people rely on polyunsaturated fat sources that contain too many omega-6 fatty acids, thus driving up their intake. You should generally aim for an intake of around 1:1 for omega-6 to omega-3 fatty acids, but many people come in closer to 10:1, even as high as 25:1 in some individuals. As you can see, this is a far cry from the 1:1 ideal that our ancestors ate that optimized their good health.

To help illustrate this point, let's look at some of the common oil sources of polyunsaturated fats and the omega-6

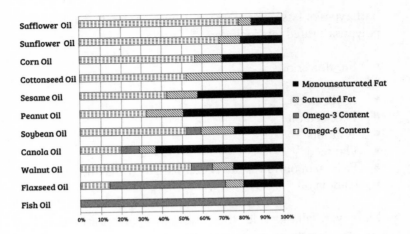

and omega-3 content of these fats. Keep in mind, other fats may come into play with these foods, but this graph specifically shows you the breakdown of the omega-3 versus omega-6 fatty acids.

As you can see, it can be quite hard to obtain a higher intake of omega-3 fatty acids without very concentrated efforts. Utilizing a fish oil supplement that contains omega-3 fatty acids will give you the best boost to help bring your intake up to where it needs to be. This is why so many people choose to supplement their diet with fish oil products. We will discuss this in greater detail in a later chapter on supplementation.

In order to help bring down your omega-6 fatty acid intake, you should be focusing on reducing your intake of corn oil, canola oil, margarine, as well as any type of hydrogenated fat. Focus instead on consuming fat sources such as virgin olive oil, walnuts and flaxseed oil, which will also provide a good dose of omega-3 fatty acids. The good news is that the amount of omega-3 fatty acids you need to eat will be directly related to how much of omega-6 fatty acids you consume as balance is required to keep the ratio in check.

Omega-3 fatty acids are also key for improving recovery rates from exercise as well as for helping you regulate your usage of carbohydrates and hence, they are an important nutrient for all exercising individuals. Remember, if you begin including polyunsaturated fats in your diet incorrectly, they will no longer be the health-boosting fats you thought they were.

Saturated Fats

Many people consume too many saturated fats in their day-to-day diet, thanks to our heavy reliance on processed, convenience and fast foods. Some amount of saturated fat in the diet is fine. It is even required as it helps to produce the cholesterol that's needed to generate your sex hormones. Remember how we spoke about men suffering from very low testosterone levels if they eat a diet that is too low in dietary fat? Well, this problem is amplified if they avoid saturated fat in particular.

Almost all sources of fat will contain at least a small dose of saturated fat, so it's not a nutrient we need to really try and consume. If you eat other healthy, fat-rich foods, you'll automatically be taking in a low level of saturated fat. To sustain optimal health, you should aim to get around 5 per cent of your total calories from saturated fats. Let's say your target food intake is 2000 calories a day. This means that no more than 100 calories should come from saturated fats, which equals around 9–10 grams total.

If you are eating the right, nutritionally dense foods, you will not exceed 10 grams of saturated fats in your diet.

So, what's so bad about saturated fats in the first place?

Foods rich in saturated fats, also come with processed carbohydrates, making the entire food item unhealthy. So it's not the saturated fat in particular that's causing the problem, but everything about the food item.

Where will you find saturated fats? The most common non-processed sources include:

- Beef
- Pork
- Mutton
- High-fat dairy products (cheese, ice cream, whole milk)
- Palm oil
- Regular butter

In addition, you will find saturated fats in a number of processed foods. Some of the major sources include:

- Pizza
- Burgers
- French fries
- Chocolate
- Baked goods (cookies, cakes, muffins)
- Processed meats
- Cream-based sauces

We need to discuss an additional type of saturated fat, which is medium chain triglyceride or MCT.

This type of saturated fat is unlike all other saturated fats and is actually very healthy for the body. This kind of fat has a slightly different chemical make-up and structure as compared to regular saturated fats. And unlike other fats, it maintains the unique property that it can be used as an immediate source of energy. So it acts very much like a carbohydrate does in the body and helps fuel intense exercise sessions. For those who are looking to eat a low-carb diet, focusing a larger number of calories on these medium chain triglycerides can help combat some of the typical fatigue felt with such an approach.

The primary source of MCT in the human diet is coconut fat and can be found in coconut oil, coconut milk, or straight-up coconut flesh. Did you ever think you could eat fats to burn fats? Well, you most certainly can.

This type of fat also has many unique health benefits. MCTs can actually boost your metabolic rate, helping keep body-fat levels in check. If you recall, when we spoke about protein earlier, we discussed the thermic effect of food. MCTs have similar properties. Each time you will consume them, you will see an increased rate in your total daily calorie burn thanks to the process of digestion. MCTs have great satiety benefits over and above what many other fats provide. This is in part due to the fact that MCTs can be used as immediate sources of energy and have no impact on your blood glucose levels. And remember, the more stable you keep your blood sugar levels, the easier it is to control hunger.

Finally, MCTs can also help improve your overall immune system's health, which helps you stay strong by reducing the chances of infections such as the common cold or flu. Maintaining a strong immune system is also key for recovering quickly from any form of exercise. Hence, medium chain triglycerides are one form of saturated fats that you do not want to avoid and do not need to count within the 5 per cent of your total calorie recommendation.

Trans Fats

Finally, the last type of dietary fat we will discuss are trans fats, which is a kind of fat that is not needed at all by the body. But, trans fats can also help you burn calories. How? Basically, if you see trans fats in food, run. Run as fast and as far away from it as you can. Run for your life. Just run! The result is that you'll burn a lot of calories by running away from them.

Trans fats are man-made and are produced when you take regular vegetable oil and put it through a process called hydrogenation. This unnatural process, of adding hydrogen to natural vegetable oils, changes the entire chemical structure of fats, making them unhealthy for consumption.

Why Do This?

Trans fats help in increasing a product's shelf-life. These types of fats are extremely stable, even at higher temperatures, so it makes it easier for companies to ship out food and then have it sit in the grocery stores for months before it reaches its expiry date. This helps corporations make more money, never mind what it's slowly doing to your body.

The bottom line is that trans fats are extremely unhealthy and the daily intake recommendation is set at zero, illustrating just how unhealthy they really are. Consuming trans fats will have you increase your levels of bad cholesterol while lowering your levels of good cholesterol, putting you at a direct risk of heart disease. Those who consume diets rich in trans fats are also more likely to develop Type 2 diabetes, thanks to increased levels of insulin resistance, and may also put themselves at a higher risk for developing cancer as well.

Trans fats do nothing good for the body, deliver absolutely no nutrition, and only make it harder to maintain healthy body weight. The best way to identify if a food contains trans fats is to simply look at the food label. In most countries, companies now need to identify if a particular food contains trans fats, so it will be listed under the main heading for fat content. Additionally, if you see the term 'partially hydrogenated vegetable oil', that's a clear indication the food contains trans fats as well.

Now, if the food does not come in a food wrapper such that there is no nutritional label to look at, you need to just use your own best judgement. If the food is deep fried, purchased from the frozen section, or in general not a healthy choice to begin with, there's a good chance it contains trans fats.

Trans fats are found most commonly in ready-to-eat foods such as:

- Pastries
- Pizza dough
- Cookies
- Crackers
- Frozen meals
- Cakes

Don't buy these foods off the shelf because it's likely they're not free of trans fats. If you make and bake these foods at home, you can use ingredients more wisely and prepare a much healthier version of these yummy snacks.

So there you have a brief look at the main types of fats that you can and do consume in your everyday diet plan. The question now remains—how much fat should you be consuming in total? In this case again, just like with carbohydrates, the total amount of dietary fat you consume will depend on how many total calories you eat throughout the course of the day, as well as how many carbohydrates you are eating overall.

You do need to maintain your calorie balance, and since protein intake is relatively fixed based on body weight, this means that the remainder of your daily calories are divided up between carbohydrates and dietary fats. You should ideally aim to consume no more than around 0.7 grams of fat per kilogram of body weight. This means that an individual weighing 75 kilograms would aim for just over 52 grams of total daily dietary fat. It's best to try and spread your dietary fat out over the course of the day as this will ensure you never end up feeling too sluggish or weighed down as you go about your day.

High-fat meals tend to sit in your stomach for hours attributed to the fact that fat digests so slowly, so this can make you feel low on energy. By focusing on eating 5–10 grams of fat per meal, based on what your specific needs are, you can avoid this from happening.

Now it's time for us to switch our focus to the micronutrients in your diet, which consist of vitamins and minerals. These are essentially found within the macronutrients that we have just talked about.

9

MICRONUTRIENTS

When it comes to nutrition, most of the focus goes to macronutrients. These big guys in nutrition tend to be what everyone talks about. How much protein to eat? Are carbohydrates really necessary? Is fat a foe? You should now have a very clear idea of what each macronutrient is all about.

That said, it's time to focus on the little guys: the micronutrients. These nutrients are hard at work each and every day, making sure that you stay healthy and feel your best. Sadly, they very rarely, if ever, get the recognition that they deserve.

Micronutrients are called 'micro' because they are needed in much smaller quantities as compared to macronutrients. They can be divided into vitamins and minerals, each of which have their own specific function. Let's look at them individually so that you get a better idea of how these come into play in your nutrition plan.

Vitamins

To get started, there are a total of thirteen essential vitamins including:

- Vitamin A
- Vitamin C

- Vitamin D
- Vitamin E
- Vitamin K
- Vitamin B1 (thiamine)
- Vitamin B2 (riboflavin)
- Vitamin B3 (niacin)
- Vitamin B6
- Vitamin B12
- Pantothenic acid
- Biotin
- Folate

Now, all of the vitamins that you take in can be grouped into two categories: fat-soluble vitamins and water-soluble vitamins. Fat-soluble vitamins are those that need to bind with fat in the stomach in order to be properly absorbed and utilized by the body. Think of the fat as a taxi that takes the

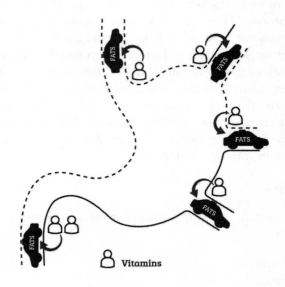

vitamin to the cells where it's needed. Without that taxi, the vitamin isn't going to get very far.

You'll often find these fat-soluble vitamins in foods that are rich in fat and other times in non-fat dense foods, which means you'll have to eat foods that are sources of these fats in order to reap full nutritional benefits. The primary fat-soluble vitamins include vitamins A, D, E and K.

For instance, kale is very rich in one fat-soluble vitamin— vitamin K—but it is quite low in dietary fat. This means that it's a very good idea to serve your kale salad with dressing made of a little olive oil so that the vitamin K can be properly utilized.

One important thing to note about these fat-soluble vitamins is that they can be stored in the body, and can, therefore, build up to toxic levels if you aren't careful. This can happen if you are overusing nutritional supplements or if you seem to have a slight obsession with a certain food. Let's say you eat a large kale salad every day for a year straight. You might start to find yourself reaching those toxic levels of vitamin K. Moderation is the key when it comes to these vitamins.

Water-soluble vitamins, on the other hand, are those that are absorbed directly by the cells, with no fat needed. This also means that they are easily flushed out of the body when not required and so the risk of toxicity is much lower as well. Since these vitamins cannot be stored in the body, if you don't consume them daily, you could risk deficiency.

It's unlikely that you will start to see any problems if you go a few days without meeting your vitamin requirements, but over the course of a few weeks, you won't be able to say the same. By this point, you may start to notice deficiency symptoms creeping in. It is also important to remember that despite the fact that these vitamins are easily washed out of the body, if you happen to take in too much, you will experience side effects such as diarrhoea. If this starts occurring and you are taking a high dose of any given vitamin, it might be time to ease up on that for a while.

So now that you have a better idea of what vitamins are, let's go through the main vitamins in terms of what they do, how many milligrams (mg) or micrograms (mcg) you need every day, and where you can find them.

Vitamins

Vitamin	Function in the Body	Required Amount	Sources
Biotin	• Required for the metabolism of proteins and carbohydrates • Helps in the production of hormones • Assists with the creation of cholesterol in the body	30 mcg/day	Cereal Dark chocolate Egg yolk Legumes Milk Nuts Pork Cooked salmon Avocado
Vitamin A	• Helps with the formation of bones and teeth • Helps build soft tissues and mucus membranes • Needed for the maintenance of healthy skin • Produces pigments in the retina of the eye • Helps promote night vision or vision in dim light • Acts as an antioxidant in the body, reducing the harmful effects of free radicals	700 mcg/day	Eggs Meat Fortified milk Cheese Cream Cod and halibut fish Sweet potato Pumpkin Cantaloupe Mango Butternut squash

Vitamin B6	• Helps with the formation of red blood cells, which help to keep your body energized during endurance activity • Assists with proper brain function • Helps to make antibodies to ward off disease and illness • Needed for maintaining proper nerve function • Creates haemoglobin • Helps with the breakdown of protein • Assists with keeping blood sugar levels in the proper range	1.3 mg/day (women) 1.7 mg/day (men)	Avocado Banana Legumes Meat Nuts Poultry Wholegrains Fortified breads and cereals
Vitamin B12	• Important for maintaining a healthy metabolism • Needed for the formation of red blood cells • Required for proper central nervous system function	2.4 mcg/day	Beef liver Shellfish Meat Poultry Eggs Milk and dairy Fortified breakfast cereals Nutritional yeast

| Vitamin C | • Necessary to support proper immune function
• Acts as an antioxidant for the body, helping reduce the harmful effects of free radicals
• Helps promote healthy teeth and gums
• Assists with the absorption of iron in the body
• Helps maintain healthy body tissues
• Promotes wound healing
• May help with recovery from physical activity
• Helps with the maintenance of cartilage
• Can reduce the severity of the common cold when taken after the on-set of the cold | 75 mg/day (women)
90 mg/day (men) | Cantaloupe
Citrus fruit (oranges and grapefruits)
Kiwi
Mango
Papaya
Pineapple
Berries (all varieties)
Watermelon
Broccoli
Brussels sprouts
Cauliflower
Green and red peppers
Sweet potato
Spinach
Cabbage
Turnip greens
Tomato
Winter squash |

Vitamin D	Helps with the absorption of calcium, therefore plays a key role in maintaining strong and healthy bones	600 IUs/day (15 mcg/day)	Direct sunlight exposure for 10–15 minutes daily
	Helps with the maintenance of healthy teeth		Fatty fish (salmon, tuna, mackerel)
	Lowers the risk factor of osteoporosis		Cheese
	May help regulate hormones in the body		Egg yolk
	Helps assist with recovery after exercise		Mushroom
	May help regulate energy levels		Fortified milk
			*Most people use a supplement for this vitamin as it can be hard to get in enough otherwise.

| Vitamin E | • Acts as an antioxidant in the body, helping to prevent free radical damage
• Helps keep skin, hair and nails healthy
• Assists with keeping the immune system strong
• Assists with the formation of red blood cells
• Makes it easier for the body to use vitamin K | 15 mg/day | Sunflower oil
Safflower oil
Corn oil
Soybean oil
Avocado
Almonds
Peanuts
Sunflower seeds
Spinach
Broccoli
Fortified cereals |

| Vitamin K | • Needed for proper blood clotting
• Plays a role in maintaining strong bones in older individuals | 90 mcg/day | Kale
Spinach
Turnip greens
Swiss chard
Parsley
Brussels sprouts
Broccoli
Cauliflower
Cabbage
Fish
Meat
Eggs |

Pantothenic acid	• Helps with the growth and development of cells in the body • Assists with the breakdown of food for use as energy • Helps manufacture cholesterol and other hormones	5 mg/day	Avocado Broccoli Kale Cabbage Eggs Legumes Lentils Milk Mushrooms Poultry Sweet potato
Niacin	• Helps ensure a healthy digestive system • Needed for proper nerve function • Assists with the development of healthy skin • Helps convert food to energy	16 mg/day (men) 14 mg/day (women)	Dairy Eggs Fish Lean meats Legumes Nuts Poultry

Nutrient	Benefits	Recommended intake	Food sources
Folic acid	• Helps with cellular growth and development • Helps to prevent birth defects when taken before pregnancy • Can help reduce the risk of suffering from anaemia	400 mcg/day (men and women) 500 mcg/day (pregnant or breastfeeding women)	Dark, leafy greens Dried beans Peas Oranges Grapefruit Kiwi
Riboflavin (vitamin B2)	• Helps work with other B vitamins to assist with energy generation and cell production • Helps with releasing energy from carbohydrates	1.3 mg/day (men) 1.1 mg/day (women)	Milk Eggs Green, leafy vegetables Lean meats Nuts Legumes
Thiamin (vitamin B1)	• Helps convert carbohydrates into energy • Helps provide energy for the brain and nervous system • Keeps muscle contractions regular	1.2 mg/day (men) 1.0 mg/day (women)	Enriched wholegrains Eggs Legumes Peas Nuts Seeds

The nutritional values in the table are based on an individual who is between eighteen- and fifty-years-old.

Feeling overwhelmed by all of this information? Don't be. The truth is that you don't need to memorize all these vitamins and the sources you can find them in. While it's good to understand how these micronutrients play a role in your body, there's no need to be able to recite them by heart. Instead, you should simply focus on eating a balanced diet with foods rich in all food groups.

As you have likely noticed in the table, vitamins are easily be found in wholegrains, meats, dairy products, nuts and seeds, along with many fruit and vegetables. If you eat natural foods from all of these categories every day, you shouldn't have too much trouble meeting your recommended intake needs.

Here's a sneaky tip. Generally speaking, the more brightly coloured a food is, especially when it comes to fruit and vegetables, the healthier it will be for you. If you can aim to eat all the colours of the rainbow each and every day, you can feel good that you're getting the nutrients that your body needs.

Now that we've discussed vitamins, let's move on to the other type of micronutrients: minerals.

Minerals

Just like vitamins, the body needs certain minerals on a daily basis in order to function optimally. These minerals are typically absorbed into the foods that you eat from the soil, which are then transferred into you. You need various minerals in different doses each day and depending on requirements, these can be denoted by the terms 'macromineral' or 'micromineral'. You'll need to take in larger quantities of macrominerals each day, while microminerals are typically only needed in trace amounts and are sometimes even referred to as trace minerals.

However, keep in mind that the amount needed of each mineral does not signal importance. Just because you may only need very small, daily doses of the microminerals does not mean that they are not essential for optimal body functioning. The main essential minerals are:

Macrominerals

- Sodium
- Chloride
- Potassium
- Calcium
- Phosphorus
- Magnesium
- Sulphur

Microminerals

- Iron
- Zinc
- Iodine
- Selenium
- Copper
- Manganese
- Fluoride
- Chromium
- Molybdenum

Let's now take a closer look at what each of these minerals does, along with the best food sources to get them from.

Mineral	Function in the Body	Required Amount	Sources
Sodium	• Needed to help maintain proper blood pressure levels • Helps keep fluid balance in the body at an optimal level • Required for proper nerve transmission • Needed for muscular contractions	2300 mg/day	Table salt Soy sauce Processed foods Canned foods Tomato-based sauces *Note that you will take in small amounts of sodium in most meats, dairy and grains
Chloride	• Helps maintain proper fluid balance in the body • Needed to maintain stomach acids necessary for digestive function	2.3 grams/day 2.0 grams/day (for those over the age of fifty)	Found along with sodium in the sources noted above

Potassium	4700 mg/day	Required for proper fluid balance Helps regulate blood pressure Helps maintain strong muscular contractions Assists with keeping the nervous system healthy	Chicken Steak Milk Banana Mango Sweet potato Beans Lentils
Calcium	1000 mg/day (men) 1200 mg/day (women)	Needed for healthy bones and teeth Required for proper muscular contractions Helps promote proper nerve function Required for adequate blood clotting Helps assist with regulating blood pressure Can help strengthen the immune system	Milk Yogurt Whey protein powder Canned fish (with bones) Fortified tofu Soy milk Broccoli Spinach Mustard greens Legumes

Phosphorus	• Needed to help promote strong bones • Keeps teeth healthy • Helps maintain a proper acid–base balance in the body	700 mg/day	Scallops Sardines Soybeans Pumpkin seeds Cod Tuna Salmon Lentils Shrimp Tempeh
Magnesium	• Stored in the bones • Required to manufacture protein in the body • Needed for optimal nerve transmission • Helps boost the immune system	400 mg/day (men) 320mg/day (women)	Pumpkin seeds Spinach Swiss chard Soybeans Sesame seeds Quinoa Black beans Cashews Sunflower seeds Navy beans

Mineral	Function	Amount	Food sources
Sulphur	• Helps with the synthesis of glutathione, one of the major antioxidants in the body • Helps with the proper maintenance of the cardiovascular and nervous systems • Binds together the two chains of amino acids that create insulin	800 mg/day	Onions Garlic Broccoli Cabbage Cauliflower Brussels sprouts Nuts Poultry Eggs Milk Legumes
Iron	• Required to help transport oxygen throughout the body in red blood cells • Needed for energy metabolism	8 mg/day (men) 18 mg/day (women) 8/day (women over fifty years in age)	Red meat Egg yolks Legumes Kale Spinach Enriched breads and cereals Shellfish

Mineral	Functions	Amount	Food sources
Zinc	• Helps create protein in the body • Required for proper taste perception • Plays a role in wound healing • Needed for foetal development • Helps with the immune system	11 mg/day (men) 8 mg/day (women)	Beef Lamb Sesame seeds Pumpkin seeds Lentils Cashews Turkey Quinoa Shrimp
Iodine	• Helps with proper thyroid function • Assists with the maintenance of the metabolic rate • Helps with proper energy development	150 mcg/day	Sea vegetables Scallops Cod Yogurt Shrimp Sardines Salmon Cow's milk Eggs Tuna

Selenium	Acts as an antioxidant in the body, minimizing free radical damage	55 mcg/day	Tuna Shrimp Sardines Salmon Turkey Cod Chicken Lamp Scallops Beef
Copper	• Needed to create various enzymes required in the body • Helps the body properly utilize iron to maintain energy for exercise	0.9 mg/day	Sesame seeds Cashew nuts Soybeans Mushrooms Sunflower seeds Tempeh Garbanzo beans Lentils Walnuts Lima beans

Manganese	• Helps assist with bone production • Keeps skin integrity intact • Helps regulate blood glucose levels and possibly prevent diabetes • Helps combat free radical damage	2.3 mg/day (men) 1.8 mg/day (women)	Cloves Oats Brown rice Garbanzo beans Spinach Pineapple Pumpkin seeds Tempeh Rye Soybeans
Fluoride	• Helps to maintain strong bones and teeth • May help prevent tooth decay	2–3 mg/day (men and women)	Seafood Tamarind
Chromium	• Helps regulate blood glucose levels along with insulin • Helps improve athletic performance	35 mcg/day (men) 24 mcg/day (women)	Broccoli Barley Oats Green beans Tomato Romaine lettuce

Molybdenum	• Helps maintain proper sulphur balance • Provides antioxidant protection • Helps maintain the nervous system • Plays a role in regulating the sleep–wake cycle	45 mcg/day	Lentils Dried peas Lima beans Kidney beans Soybeans Black beans Oats Barley

The nutritional values in the table above are based on an individual who is between eighteen- and fifty-years-old.

Once again, don't stress if this seems like too much to remember. If you eat a diet that's rich in a wide variety of different foods, you should have no problem meeting your needs for most nutrients. If you are restricting your diet in any way, due to allergies or by following fad diets, then it becomes important to identify if you are potentially missing out on any nutrients and taking steps to eliminate those deficiencies. In most cases, this can easily be done with a vitamin, multivitamin or mineral supplement. However, before taking any such dietary supplements, you must consult a nutritionist or a general physician to know how much of each vitamin or mineral you should be consuming as per your requirements.

Now let's move forward and discuss the last and perhaps the most important element of proper nutrition: hydration.

10

WATER FOR SURVIVAL AND BEYOND

As an athlete, it is critically important that you constantly pay attention to being adequately hydrated. Whenever you exercise, you will be increasing water loss through all the sweating. Even if you feel like you are not sweating that hard during your training, make no mistake about it, you will still be losing a great deal of water. And this water needs to be replaced. If you go into a training session even slightly dehydrated, even as little as 1–2 per cent (for instance, if you have not consumed any fluids in the three hours before starting training or you're starting your workout on a dry mouth), it can have a detrimental impact on your performance.

Let's look at why proper hydration is so important so that you can understand all the many reasons to start paying attention to it.

Blood Pressure Regulation

The very first reason you must stay hydrated is to help maintain proper blood pressure levels. Small amounts of dehydration can mean that you have less total blood volume circulating throughout your body, which then not only places more stress on your heart to pump this blood around, but also means there is less pressure exerted on your arteries. This, in turn, results in lower blood pressure overall.

Those who are suffering from low blood pressure are more likely to start feeling dizzy and they may just pass out, which, as you can imagine, is hardly a good thing as far as keeping up with your athletic performance is concerned. While you definitely don't want very high blood pressure levels, you also don't want to have levels that are too low either.

Energy Levels

Next, you need to think about your energy levels. A low fluid intake, as noted, can really influence your overall energy levels. This isn't applicable to just your energy level during exercise only but applies to your day-to-day living as well. If you constantly feel like you're dragging yourself through the day, check your hydration status. Dehydration may be to blame for your low energy levels.

Metabolic Rate

If you aren't drinking enough fluids throughout the day, this can also slow down your metabolic rate, making it harder to maintain body weight. Low water intake can cause water retention, as the body will not let go of the fluids. Also, many times, thirst is misunderstood as hunger. In order to prevent yourself from eating 'unwanted' foods, make sure your water intake is substantial. Sluggish metabolic rates will also lead to lower energy levels, having negative consequences on your athletic performance.

Appetite Regulation

Appetite regulation is another benefit of staying hydrated. Many people often mistake thirst for hunger, eating when they really just need a drink of water. If you do this regularly, you'll quickly find yourself gaining excess body fat due to the incoming calories that you just don't need. Ensuring you drink a tall glass of water before every meal or snack will help you avoid making this error.

Reduced Joint Pain

As someone involved in athletic training, joint pain is something you definitely don't want getting you down. Sadly though, if you aren't hydrating properly, it just may happen. Staying well hydrated will help keep your cartilage soft, reducing any pain associated with the grinding of bones. Proper hydration will also help keep your joints as lubricated as possible, reducing the chances of pain in that regard as well. Hydration is very important to bear in mind while trying to prevent injuries from sports training.

Cleanse the Body

Let's not forget the fact that staying properly hydrated is also a great way to help cleanse your body. The incoming water will help to remove any toxic waste build-up in your system, while also flushing out unwanted bacteria. Those who are not hydrating themselves on a regular basis are more prone to falling ill and may even be at a greater risk of suffering from disease. You don't want to compromise your immunity when you decide to train like a pro.

Brain Function

Finally, your brain also needs plenty of water for optimal functioning. Even small amounts of dehydration can lead to headaches and cloudy thinking, causing you to feel unwell. Those who find they have trouble focusing during the day may also be showing signs of dehydration, so drinking a tall glass of water will help combat this.

So as you can see, there are many reasons for staying hydrated that go beyond simply improving your sports performance and decreasing your thirst for drinking fluids throughout the day.

When it comes to what you choose to hydrate yourself with, water is almost always the best choice. Water is completely pure and natural for the body and since it doesn't contain any calories at all, consumption won't impact body weight. During times of high-endurance activity, in which you are sweating quite heavily, you may wish to consider an electrolyte replacement beverage, which contains the sodium and potassium to help you sustain proper blood pressure. We'll discuss this in detail shortly.

So How Much Water Do You Need?

Your ideal water intake will vary every day depending on the activity that you are doing. The days that you are more active, you'll need more water to replenish lost fluids. Generally speaking, aim to drink around half your body weight (in kilograms) in fluid ounces. So if you weigh around 70 kilograms, you would need to drink around 35 ounces. Here's a simple conversion table to keep in mind.

1 ounce = 30 millilitres
35 ounces = 1050 millilitres

That means that you need to consume approximately 1 litre of water every day. Note that this amount is for maintenance purposes, assuming you are not exercising and living in a non-humid climate. However, for every fifteen minutes that you spend doing intense exercise (or out in direct sunlight or heat), add one additional cup of water or 200 millilitres to that amount.

Another very effective way to determine how much water to drink to replace water loss during exercise is to weigh yourself before the exercise session and then weigh yourself after you are finished. You can estimate an additional one litre of fluid for every kilogram of body weight that you've lost during the exercise session. So hypothetically, if you were 2 kilograms lighter after your workout, this means you would need to drink 2 litres of water.

You might also wonder whether you can simply listen to thirst as your guide for how much and how often you should drink water. Will drinking fluids simply when you are thirsty keep you adequately hydrated? For some people this works just fine, but for others, not as much. Usually, by the time you are physically feeling thirst, you are already in a state of partial dehydration. Thus, you are now playing catch-up to get to where you want to be. Instead, developing the habit of drinking at regular intervals throughout the day is a wiser move.

An alternative strategy to listening to your thirst is to look at the colour of your urine. While this may seem odd, it's a practical indication of how hydrated you are. If your urine is any darker than a pale yellow colour, it's an indication that you need to be drinking more water. Your urine doesn't necessarily have to be completely clear since that suggests you are taking in too much water, but it shouldn't be bright yellow either. Keep in mind that taking certain vitamins can make your urine a bright yellow too.

In addition to these points, here are a few other tips to know and remember while meeting your hydration requirements:

- Keep a water bottle with you at all times to drink from throughout the day.
- Try adding some freshly sliced fruit or cucumber to a pitcher of water to add a hint of flavour, making it easier to go down.
- Drink a tall glass of water before each and every meal.
- Start meals with a broth-based soup, as this will count towards your hydration intake.
- Sip on hot, herbal tea if you want, since it will count as a serving of water.

While it may seem challenging to get your hydration needs met, once you start putting these tips into place and becoming more aware of your intake, you'll find it's far easier than you initially thought to keep yourself hydrated.

You Can Get Too Much of a Good Thing

Before we move on to the next chapter, you do need to know that an increased water intake is not always beneficial. With hydration, you can get too much of a good thing. The problem with drinking too much water is that it can cause the electrolytes in your body (sodium and potassium) to become very diluted, resulting in low blood pressure, dizziness and feelings of weakness.

Overhydration is also a very real issue and something that all those participating in athletic activities should be aware of. If you are exercising outdoors on a hot summer's day, you may find that your thirst is almost insatiable. In these cases, where you are drinking a lot of fluids, you'll want to consider using an electrolyte replacement beverage instead. This way, you will maintain the proper level of sodium and potassium in the body while still meeting your hydration needs.

It's easy to put much of the focus of good nutrition on your food intake, looking closely at your calorie consumption and the macronutrients you're taking in, but hydration can be just as important—if not more important. While you can go for days without food and still survive, you cannot go for much longer without water.

Before we wrap up our section on nutrition, let's finish talking specifically about recovery nutrition and what you should be doing to ensure you come out of each exercise session feeling as strong as possible.

11

RECOVERY NUTRITION 101

Whenever you are participating in intense physical activity, you are going to be placing heavy demands on the body—demands that it then must deal with. You'll be breaking down body tissues, causing your muscles to grow weaker as your workout continues, which then, after recovery, is what will allow them to grow back stronger than they were before. This said, in order for that growth to occur, you need to supply your body with the raw materials to do so.

This is where nutrition comes into play. While what you eat over the next twenty-four to forty-eight hours will definitely help with improving recovery rates, the time period right after your workout session is especially critical as this is when your body is ready to take in any nutrients it's fed and put them to work immediately.

So what do you need for recovery? Let's take a quick look.

Fast-acting Protein

The very first thing that you'll need to eat immediately following your training session is a fast-acting source of protein. Right after training, your muscles are in a broken-down state. Picture this. Your house has just caught fire and the very place you live is being destroyed. Would you want the fire truck to take the longest route possible to your house or would you want it to go directly there, as quickly as possible?

Clearly, when your home is at stake, you want them there NOW. The longer they take, the longer it'll take for you to rebuild your home because the damage from the fire will just worsen the longer it burns. The same goes for your muscles after a workout session. The sooner you can get the repair team—the protein—to those muscle tissues, the sooner the rebuilding process can start. This means there will be less for you to rebuild or repair later on, allowing you to recover that much faster between workout sessions.

Which protein is best then? For the absolute most optimal results, you'll want to go with a whey isolate protein powder. This particular type of whey protein has been designed to digest as rapidly as possible and will serve your needs perfectly in this situation. Whey is also quick and easy, so there's no need to waste precious time cooking as you would with food protein. You simply measure it out, mix with water, shake and drink.

If you don't want to use whey or don't have any around, the next best options include egg whites or white fish. While these still won't break down nearly as fast as the whey isolate would, they'll break down faster than chicken or paneer.

How much protein you need to consume immediately after training will depend on:

- Your current body weight
- Your total calorie intake
- How intense and long your workout session was

The heavier you are and the longer and more intensely you are training, the higher your protein intake will need to be.

Likewise, the lower the calories in your diet, the more protein you will need as there is a higher risk that your body will be in a catabolic state. This means your body is breaking down muscle tissue at an accelerated pace instead of building it.

Just to give you an idea, most athletes will be best served taking in between 25–50 grams of protein post their workouts. This is like taking one scoop of whey protein isolate or three whole eggs.

Simple Carbohydrates

In addition to fast-acting protein, you also want to take in some simple carbohydrates after your workout. Now, the information I am about to present to you is exactly the opposite of what we have already discussed, so pay close attention so that you fully understand the concept.

During the day, your main mission with your carbohydrate intake should be to stabilize blood glucose levels. You never want to create a sharp increase in blood glucose as this will cause a high amount of insulin to be released from the pancreas, which will then promote the accumulation of body fat storage with those carbohydrates now in the body.

Post workout, however, this is precisely what you want. At this point, because you've just completed a training session, you won't be moving the carbohydrates into the body fat cells but into your muscle glycogen stores instead. Picture your muscle cell as a large fuel tank. Before your workout, it was filled up, ready to be used. Immediately following the workout, the muscle cell has been emptied and is now completely dry.

When you spike blood glucose levels (by eating simple carbohydrates), you'll release insulin, and insulin is like a bus that carries all those carbohydrates into the tank, filling it up so it's ready for the next time. If you don't get that large release of insulin, eventually those glucose molecules will find their way to the muscle cells, but it will take a lot longer. They're walking to the tank rather than being driven.

And spiking blood glucose does another thing: it'll also help shuttle faster the protein that you eat into the muscle cells. So if you eat a fast-digesting source of protein plus spike blood glucose levels, you're really putting your best foot forward for a maximum recovery.

So which simple carbs are best post workout and how many?

When we say simple carbs, fruit works very well here as simple sugar is found in most fruit. Alternatively, white rice, white potatoes, white bread, or even some rice cakes can work too. The key thing you want to ensure is that any carbohydrate you choose is low in fats. If there is too much fat in the carbohydrate, it will blunt the spike in blood glucose levels and throw the entire series of events off-kilter. Think of fat as a handbrake on the bus, slowing it down completely.

Therefore, low-fat carbs are best here. Again, how many carbs you need will heavily depend on the duration and intensity level of your training session. The more intense the session, the more fuel you will need to get through it, and thus, the more drained your 'tank' will be. Those who have more total body weight will also require more carbohydrates simply because they have a larger tank that needs to be filled. A good general rule? Aim for around 0.4 grams of carbs per kilogram of body weight per twenty minutes of intense exercise training.

So if you weigh 55 kilograms, for instance, and did a workout that was an hour long, you would want to consume about 66 grams of carbohydrates in total, or just over 250 calories worth. This will help replenish the energy that you used while also providing your body with energy to utilize the protein that you ate to assemble new, lean muscle mass tissue.

Try and take both your protein and carbohydrates together, if possible. Some great ideas for post-exercise meals are:

- A whey protein isolate shake made with bananas or some orange juice
- Boiled egg whites with white potatoes
- Grilled fish served with white rice
- A soy protein isolate shake and some white bread smeared with a little jam

As long as your meal of choice meets the requirements noted above, you'll be setting up your recovery meals correctly. So there you have the foundational concepts that you need to know about proper nutrition for sports training. If you want to become an athlete, you need to make sure that you are putting the right fuel in your engine—it's that simple.

Now let's move to our next section, which discusses sports supplementation in greater detail.

PART IV

SUPPLEMENTS

By now, you have understood how to fuel your body for athletic training and how to prepare your lifestyle to ensure optimal success. It's time to look at how to best use supplements in order to meet your nutritional needs.

12

SMART SUPPLEMENTS

There are literally thousands of different supplements you can choose from, and many of these will just burn a hole in your wallet without offering you very many benefits or worse, they can potentially put you at risk for unwanted side effects! However, if you do choose the right one, it can really pay off. Well-chosen supplements can give you that extra edge and can take an athlete from being good to being a truly great one.

But you need to have the basics down first. First and foremost, tend to your nutrition and training programme. Only once you feel confident you are doing everything you should as regards your nutrition should you begin to consider taking supplements. Too many people make the grave mistake of jumping into supplements too early on, thinking that doing so will make up for not eating or exercising properly.

Remember, supplements are called *supplements* for a reason. They are going to *supplement* your training and nutrition programme, not replace it. Don't ever expect them to. If you go in with accurate expectations of what a supplement can do and work hard while using it, you will

have great results. Let's begin by talking about some of the
main types of supplements.

Macronutrient Supplements

The very first type of supplements to consider are the
macronutrient supplements, referring to those that
contain protein, carbohydrates or fats—the three primary
macronutrients needed in large quantities.

　　Let's evaluate each individually:

Protein

Protein supplements are very popular in the athletic and
training world because your protein needs increase when
doing heavy training and supplements make it easy to meet
your protein requirements. Now, people usually fall into one
of two camps when talking about protein supplements. You
have the first group who swear by them and use them often
and the second who believe protein supplements may be
dangerous and/or unhealthy. Which group is right?

　　First, you must realize that protein supplements are just
a fast and easy way to consume protein. Provided it is a
high-quality protein supplement you are using, it's not going
to be much different for your body than eating chicken
breast or some fish. Both sources provide you with the raw
material you need to rebuild and repair muscle tissue.

　　That said, there are certain micronutrients found
in whole foods that you simply won't get from a protein
supplement, and so you should never replace all your food
choices with supplements. But having one or two protein
shakes per day is a perfectly healthy way to get your needs
met. Additionally, too much protein—over and beyond
recommended dosage—is not necessary. If you are drinking

protein shakes like you drink water, it's completely useless. And technically, you would never need so much protein anyway. Always remember, excess protein gets converted into fat.

Now that we've dispelled this myth, let's talk about the various protein supplements:

Whey Powder

Whey protein powder is the most common type of protein supplement. This powder is a form of dairy products, and will typically also provide you with calcium. A basic whey protein powder digests quickly and contains immunoglobulins, which will help to strengthen your immune system and keep you feeling your best. Many people don't realize this about protein powder, but drinking a protein shake could actually help you feel healthier overall. In addition to this, whey tends to blunt your appetite. So for athletes who are seeking to control their weight, they may find that they eat less on days they have whey protein.

Whey Isolate Powder

One specific type of protein, whey isolate protein, is derived from whey but has been designed to digest as rapidly as possible in the body. You may recall this being mentioned in the post-workout nutrition section. Whey isolate protein powder is ideally consumed immediately after your workout. It'll get the necessary amino acids into the muscle cells as quickly as possible, ensuring that you have a prompt and smooth recovery.

Whey isolate protein powder is also very easy to mix in a shaker cup, which makes it excellent for taking with you to wherever you are training. This protein powder is typically very low in both fat and carbs, making it a clean source of lean protein.

Casein Powder

Another form of protein powder, casein protein, has been designed to do the opposite of whey isolate. While whey isolate digests rapidly, casein protein digests very slowly. For this reason, it's typically used by athletes before they go to bed, if they want to provide their body with a source of protein that will last them until morning.

This protein powder can also be used throughout the day, if you know that it'll be quite some time before you get the chance to eat another meal. This protein should not be consumed too close to a workout, however, as it's simply too slow-digesting to be truly beneficial.

Hemp, or Soy Powder

For those who do not consume dairy, either because they are lactose intolerant or because they are vegans, you can consider hemp or soy protein powder options. Both of these are vegan-friendly and provide you with an excellent source of protein as well. However, men should stick with hemp protein powder as soy protein can exert unwanted effects on their overall sex hormone balance, lowering testosterone and increasing oestrogen levels.

Soy also interferes with thyroid hormones. People suffering from hypothyroidism should not eat too much soy and its products as part of their daily meal plan. Hemp protein powder will also provide some additional omega-3 fatty acids, which provide greater benefits than just being a fast and easy source of protein. Women can choose either of these as alternatives to whey protein.

Meal Replacement Powder

Finally, the last type of protein powder that you could consider is a meal replacement powder. These are unlike other protein powders in that they also provide you with some carbohydrates and fats in addition to the protein and are designed for people who can't eat normal meals because they are travelling or don't have access to food. You take meal replacement powders to replace a typical meal or snack.

While these would be better than, say, grabbing a chocolate bar from a vending machine, try not to rely on them. They lack the dietary fibre and micronutrients you would get from whole foods; they aren't very satisfying and they may contain unwanted added sugars as well. They can be used as a last resort, but don't use them more often than that.

So there you have a closer look into the various protein powder supplements that you can choose from. Now let's talk about carbohydrate supplement options.

Carbohydrates

For some individuals, especially endurance athletes such as marathoners, carbohydrate supplementation is important.

If you are aiming to build more lean muscle mass, adding a carbohydrate supplement to your post-workout protein shake could help give you the extra boost and calories you need to really kick-start the process of protein synthesis (muscle building).

What options do you have for carbohydrate supplements? Here are the main ones to consider:

Waxy Maize

The first of the available carbohydrate supplements is a substance called waxy maize. This carbohydrate source has been designed to allow for optimal absorption rates, getting it into your muscle tissues where it's needed and ensuring full recovery from athletic exercise. It can also act as a shuttle for other supplements that you may be taking, such as creatine, helping these substances move into the muscle tissues faster and making them more effective.

Waxy maize is completely animal-free, making it a great option for vegetarians and as it comes in powdered form, it is quick and easy to use immediately after your workout. It is made from corn, which is a starch that delivers energy over an extended period of time. This helps ensure that after consuming waxy maize, you won't suffer from a crash shortly after exercise as your energy levels drop. Instead, you'll sustain an even keel over time.

Karbolyn

Another carbohydrate supplement option is Karbolyn, a form of waxy maize designed to offer faster absorption rates and yet help sustain energy over a longer period of time as compared to pure sugar. Many people who need faster recovery rates—for instance, if you are training twice per day or participating in two separate matches or races in one day—will want to use Karbolyn as this will help them recover even faster than if they were using waxy maize. On the plus side, you won't get that crash that typical glucose results in and hence, Karbolyn will leave you feeling better overall.

Dextrose

Dextrose is a carbohydrate supplement that comes in powdered form and can be mixed with your protein powder as well. Dextrose is a simpler carb as compared to the previous two options, so it will also offer that rapid spike in blood glucose levels but will also leave you crashing down from that quite rapidly. Now you might be wondering, why would you want that?

In some cases, athletes may choose to use dextrose if they are doing a very short duration event or training session and they know that their training session will be followed by a more wholesome meal, containing slower digesting carbohydrates. This way they get the immediate spike in blood glucose from the dextrose as their blood sugar starts to fall, and then they'll be able to immediately turn to the next meal they are eating to provide sustenance and balance those blood glucose levels out.

Some people report simply feeling better and more energized with dextrose and so, in that case, it may be the superior option to Karbolyn and waxy maize.

Energy Gels

Finally, there are energy gels. Energy gels are typically used by those who perform endurance events. In composition these are pretty much purely carbohydrates. These are faster-acting carbohydrates that will provide a source of energy when the athlete feels like they have reached a point of complete exhaustion (also known as bonking), giving them a pick-me-up so as to continue with the event.

There are a great many different brands of energy gels available, so you should do a little research to find the one that works for you. Most of these gels contain between 25–60 grams of carbs, and also contain some of the important electrolytes, including potassium and sodium. Some gels may also contain caffeine to give you an additional pick-me-up. As they aren't in liquid form, many runners find energy gels sit better in their stomachs and don't leave them suffering from cramps shortly after. In addition to gels, you may also find chews on the market as well, which act in the same way as gels but have a slightly different texture.

Some athletes will choose to supplement with carbohydrates while others won't do so at all. The choice is entirely yours and will greatly depend on what you are doing for your diet, your energy needs and how you react to these products. However, while training for a sport, almost everyone should consider using a protein powder supplement as this has been proven greatly beneficial time and again.

Now let's take a closer look at the micronutrient supplements you might consider taking as well.

Micronutrient Supplements

Micronutrient supplements simply refer to the vitamins and minerals that you may choose to include in your supplementation plan. If you know, for instance, that your diet is falling short in a particular vitamin or mineral, adding a supplement to make up for this deficiency can help you offset any potential negative health side effects that you otherwise would experience.

Remember though, it's almost always better to get your nutrients from real food whenever possible. So don't think that you can just pop a supplement and sit back and eat unhealthy food all day long. That isn't the way to go about it. Instead, these vitamin and mineral supplements should only be used if you are trying to eat right, but still coming up short.

For instance, if you suffer from lactose intolerance and can't have any dairy products as a result of it, you may want to consider adding a calcium supplement into your diet plan. This will help ensure that you are fostering strong bone growth and development and preventing stress fractures or osteoporosis.

Likewise, iron supplements should be considered because it is necessary to ensure proper red blood cell formation and the transfer of oxygen throughout the body and specifically to the exercising muscle tissue. If you start to fall low in your red blood cell count—and suffer from anaemia as a result—you could begin to fatigue easily during your workout sessions.

While you can just take a good quality multivitamin and multimineral supplement, if you are eating a very balanced diet, you may not need all these additional nutrients and would be better served by taking individual supplements instead. Some of the common vitamins and minerals athletes should consider using supplements for include:

- Calcium: To promote strong bone growth and development
- Magnesium: To promote deeper sleep and recovery, elevated testosterone, increased protein synthesis and reduced inflammation
- Vitamin D: To help improve bone health, strengthen the immune system and increase natural testosterone release
- Iron: To support higher energy during activity and delay fatigue
- Vitamin C: To support the immune system and help speed recovery post exercise
- Vitamin B Complex: To ensure optimal energy levels on a day-to-day basis
- Zinc: To help increase the level of natural testosterone release, improving strength and power
- Selenium: To improve immunity and recovery
- Chromium: To increase muscle mass and regularize insulin levels

This list includes the most commonly used supplements that you should consider, but do keep in mind that you should do a full assessment of your diet to see where you stand on all the vitamins and minerals that we discussed earlier.

Hydration Supplements

The next category of supplements to consider is hydration supplements, which serve to hydrate you while providing additional benefits. You can think of them as super drinks. These are often collectively called sports drinks and are mistaken for energy drinks. However, energy drinks and sports drinks are two very different things.

Energy drinks are beverages that are typically used by the average individual to boost their energy on a day when they are feeling particularly tired. These drinks usually contain a high dose of sugar along with other energizing ingredients such as caffeine, green tea extract, B vitamins and taurine. Red Bull is a very popular example of an energy drink. While these can be used to give you a burst of energy for your workout if you wish, they are not designed for the purpose.

Sports drinks, on other hand, such as Gatorade and Powerade, have been custom-made to address the exercise demands of an athlete. These drinks will often also contain carbohydrates, typically as glucose, with sugar or calorie-free varieties available. For those athletes who are watching their body weight or carbohydrate intake, the latter options would be preferable.

But more importantly, sports drinks contain important electrolytes (sodium, potassium and chloride), which help you sustain greater physical activity. Remember that when you sweat, you aren't just losing water. You are actually sweating out salt and potassium as well. If this salt and potassium is not replaced and you continue to sweat quite heavily, it can eventually begin to interfere with your performance and even your cognition. Those who lose too much of these electrolytes and only replace the fluid loss with plain water will begin to see such diluted levels of electrolytes in their body that they can suffer from something called hyponatremia (a condition where the sodium content in the blood is dangerously low). The symptoms of hyponatremia are:

- Feelings of nausea and potentially vomiting
- Ongoing headaches
- Feeling confused and/or disoriented
- Seeing your energy level decline and high levels of fatigue set in
- Suffering from muscle weakness and/or cramping

If untreated long enough and it gets very serious, this condition can, in fact, lead to seizures and coma. Sports drinks are designed to combat this. They contain the perfect ratio of sodium and potassium that should be naturally found in your bloodstream. So when you hydrate with these beverages, you will ensure that you are staying within safe ranges.

In addition to the two primary electrolytes, sodium and potassium, many sports drinks also contain small amounts of magnesium, chloride and calcium, which are also needed to sustain optimal muscular contractions during exercise. While you won't need these micronutrients to the same degree as you need sodium and potassium, if their levels start to run too low, it can impact performance as well. You can typically find sports drinks in either pre-made, ready-to-drink forms or in powdered form, which you can then simply mix with water yourself.

Taking care of your hydration needs with proper supplements is important. While someone who is playing a thirty-minute match of badminton is likely going to be fine hydrating with just water, a marathoner heading out for a three-hour run is going to need a lot more. You should know the requirements and demands of your sport and training to plan ahead and address these demands accordingly.

Remember, sports drinks and gels are high in simple sugars and consuming them for a less than thirty-minute, low-to-moderate intensity workout, or just as a style statement, is of no benefit. Rather, it will have negative consequences because the excess sugar will get converted to fat and your body will not use the stored fat as energy.

Ergogenic Supplements

Now it's time to talk about ergogenic supplements, which literally means to enhance work capacity. These supplements help to enhance performance giving you that extra edge needed to achieve your personal best. These are the legal, performance-boosting supplements that you can use to help get more out of your athletic training.

Each supplement is going to bring about different benefits, so it is important to consider which supplement will best address your workout and sport performance goals. Let's go over the most commonly used ergogenic supplements and how they will benefit you.

Creatine

The first and one of the most commonly used ergogenic aids is creatine monohydrate. You may have heard of this before, as it is so very popular among any strength-focused athletes or those required to exert short bursts of force during their sport of choice. Creatine monohydrate serves as the precursor to the high-energy compound ATP. Creatine also helps ensure that your body is fully saturated in creatine monohydrate, so that it can effectively form ATP to keep those muscular contractions going.

Some people mistakenly believe that creatine itself will help you build muscle and gain weight. However, this is not the case. All creatine does is help you work harder and longer in the gym, and it's that sort of hard work that will then help you experience increased performance and strength and muscle gains. If you just take creatine on its own and don't exercise, don't expect to see any strength gains at all.

Generally speaking, creatine is quite safe to take and minor side effects such as some temporary water retention may occur when you first begin using it. This can usually be offset, however, by increasing your water intake when first starting it. When using creatine, you can either choose to take 5 grams per day before or after your workout, where you'll eventually reach that level of full saturation in the muscle cells, or you can choose to do a loading phase, taking four servings of 5 grams each throughout the day for five days straight. After that's over, you can then move into the normal 3–5 gram per day phase.

Either approach will work. It all depends on how fast you want to become saturated with creatine and whether you can deal with some temporary water retention associated with the loading phase.

BCAAs

The next ergogenic aid to consider is BCAAs, which stands for Branched Chain Amino Acids, and refers to three particular amino acids: L-Valine, L-Leucine and L-Isoleucine.

These particular amino acids bypass the liver and move directly into the muscle cells, where they can be used for energy as well as to prevent large amounts of muscle tissue breakdown. Using BCAAs supplements either before or during your workout (many people will choose to sip on them during their workout as BCAAs are mixed with water and taste absolutely delicious!) will help you feel stronger during your sessions and may help you recover faster between workout sessions than you otherwise would have.

BCAAs are also important to use if you ever plan to do any form of exercise without eating first. While it's generally not recommended to ever attempt a workout or training session without eating, if it's a shorter, low-intensity workout, you could do it before breakfast. However to prevent muscle mass loss, using these BCAAs would be helpful. BCAAs typically come in a number of different flavour options and can also be a great way to encourage yourself to stay well hydrated during exercise as they transform bland water into quite a flavourful beverage.

Caffeine

The next ergogenic aid is one that is also very commonly used: caffeine. You will typically find caffeine in any pre-workout products in the market, or it can be taken on its own in tablet form (or by drinking a plain old cup of coffee). Caffeine serves multiple different purposes.

Caffeine is a fantastic way to improve your energy levels. You already know this if you wake up to the smell of coffee each morning (and would never manage without it). Moderate doses of caffeine can take you from feeling rather tired to feeling very energized and ready to go. In addition, caffeine is also excellent for enhancing mental focus and drive, which will give an additional edge to your performance.

Caffeine can also help increase fat burning in the body, and for those athletes who are concerned about maintaining a lean body composition to improve their performance, this is another crucial element. It is important to note that caffeine can lead to some unwanted side effects depending on how sensitive you are and how much you consume.

Firstly, you should avoid taking any caffeine-containing product too close to bedtime as it will interfere with sleep.

Secondly, ensure that you consider cutting back on other substances containing caffeine to balance your daily total. You should aim to stay around the 200–300 mg per day mark to avoid becoming too dependent on caffeine or suffering from other unwanted side effects.

Those who take too much caffeine tend to experience jitteriness, racing heart rates, anxiety and may find that they are rather shaky in their movements—nothing of which will benefit you as an athlete. So while you can consider caffeine supplements, be smart about how you use them.

Caffeine is known by many other names including coffee extract, tea extract, 1,3,7-Trimethylxanthine, anhydrous caffeine, cafeina, caffeine sodium benzoate, caffeine citrate, caffeine methylxanthine, cuarana and Liquid Crack. If you see any of these names on a product label, know that you are pretty much getting caffeine.

Ephedrine

Now we come to an ergogenic product that has received a lot of negative attention. The chances are that you've heard of this before and have already formed negative connotations in association with it: ephedrine, ma huang or just ephedra for short. Ephedrine is a herbal ingredient that stimulates the central nervous system, increasing heart rate, blood pressure, energy levels and overall metabolic rate. It's also often used in diet drugs since it has you burning more energy on an hourly basis after taking it.

The problem with ephedrine is that an overdose poses a serious threat to your health, as it can put you at risk for heart attacks. While some athletes still choose to use it, often pairing it with caffeine (the two are almost always taken together), you need to tread lightly with this supplement. It can do more harm than good so if you are going to use it, be sure that you use a very low dosage to start with to check for reactions and then build up from there.

Also note that if you see the term 'bitter orange' on a food label, know it is a substance similar to ephedrine, but a more natural version of it. Regardless, tread carefully with any products containing that as well.

Beta-Alanine

The next ergogenic ingredient that you will often find in products designed to improve performance is Beta-Alanine, which offers powerful benefits to those who use it in their pre-workout products. Beta-Alanine works as a buffer in the muscles and delays cramping during intense activities.

You know that burning sensation you typically feel when doing a high-repetition set of leg extensions, for instance? This is due to the formation of hydrogen ions. Beta-Alanine, by raising carnosine levels, can help reduce the build-up of hydrogen ions and thus reduce that burning feeling—meaning you can keep going for longer.

While using Beta-Alanine supplements, note that you will feel a sort of tingly sensation in the body, which indicates that the supplement is working. This isn't something to be alarmed at as it will cause no harm to you. If you really dislike that tingly sensation, you can avoid it by breaking your doses of Beta-Alanine into smaller ones, taking them multiple times through the day rather than taking one large dose all at once. Beta-Alanine is often paired with creatine as together they help to combat fatigue, giving you the best possible benefits to keep up the intensity of your training longer.

Citrulline Malate

Citrulline malate is another ingredient designed to help you combat fatigue during exercise, this time by decreasing the level of ammonia created during intense exercise. Ammonia is a waste product produced during protein breakdown, which intensifies during exercise and needs to be excreted from the system. Ammonia is a key player in causing fatigue and if too much of it builds up in the system, beyond the human body's capacity to excrete it, you may exhaust yourself to the extent of discontinuing your exercise any further.

In addition to that, citrulline malate is known to help increase the quantity of nitric oxide. What does nitric oxide do? Having higher amounts of nitric oxide in your bloodstream will cause the blood vessels to dilate, which in turn can increase blood flow to the working muscle tissues. Since your blood is going to bring both nutrients and oxygen to the working muscle cells, this helps them work harder while reducing the level of fatigue experienced.

In addition, the increased blood flow also gives you that pumped up feeling you may get when doing strength training activities. While this won't necessarily help performance directly, it can help increase your overall rate of lean muscle mass building and for some, it can be quite motivational to keep working hard. Seeing your muscles enlarged and pumped up like that can trigger you to keep up the hard work as you see direct results of your training session.

The increased blood flow to the muscle tissues will also help to improve recovery rates. So you might find that you bounce back faster between training sessions. The more frequently you train, the faster you will see progress.

Taurine

Taurine, yet another amino acid, is also sometimes added to products to be used before a workout as it can help increase your levels of mental focus and energy. Going into a training session feeling ready to give it your all can really help the outcome of that session because it will ensure that you are performing at your very best.

Taurine is also important for protein synthesis to take place, so including it into your supplement protocol could help your body make better use of the protein powder you're using, ensuring optimal protein synthesis. As taurine is a natural substance that you will take in through food sources as well, there is little to no risk of side effects.

Vitamin B12

Vitamin B12 is another natural ingredient that is sometimes added into pre-workout products or taken alone on its own. High doses of this vitamin can amplify energy levels significantly, giving you energy comparable to what you would get with caffeine without the central nervous system stimulation. For those who are sensitive to caffeine and would prefer not to use it regularly (or those who train in the evenings), vitamin B12 can serve as a great replacement. While it may not be quite as powerful as caffeine, it can be healthier option for some people.

Glutamine

Glutamine is an ergogenic amino acid that can also be taken daily through food. Large doses of glutamine can help support optimal immune system function. As your immune system plays a key role in the recovery rates between workouts, glutamine can help you get back at your training quicker. Each workout you do will impact your immune system in a negative way by tearing it down, and so, doing all you can to build it back up again is important. Those who train too heavily may often find that they fall ill quite frequently and this is evidence of a weakened immune system. By using glutamine, they can prevent this from happening.

So there you have a closer look at the primary ergogenic and pre-workout ingredients you can use. You can either take these on their own, or as is more common, in a blended product typically referred to as a pre-workout supplement. While shopping for a pre-workout supplement, make sure that you read the list of ingredients carefully so you know precisely what you are consuming. Each pre-workout product will have a different mixture of ingredients in it and will impact you in a different manner. Take the time to ensure that whichever you choose to use is going to be optimal for your needs.

Now let's move on to fat-burning supplements.

Fat-burning Supplements

The last category of supplements that you are likely to come across is fat burners, which, as the name suggests, are designed to help you burn fat. These supplements also typically contain a mixture of different ingredients, each to achieve a specific goal. The primary purpose of fat-burning supplements is to:

- Increase energy levels (which are generally lower when on a low-calorie diet plan)
- Increase metabolic rate (which allows you to burn more fat daily)
- Decrease hunger levels (which makes it easier to stick to your reduced calorie diet)

Since these are the areas that people struggle with the most while aiming to lose fat, if a product can give you a leg up on these things, it can certainly help you see success. Caffeine, guarana, bitter orange and ephedrine are the most commonly used products in fat-burning supplements, and so you'll typically see these ingredients on the label (in one combination or another).

Fat-burning products may also use:

- CLA (conjugated linoleic acid): This is a particular fatty acid that may help increase the body's usage of fat as a fuel source, giving you better overall fat-loss results.
- *Hoodia gordonii*: This is a particular herb used to help decrease appetite levels considerably, making it far easier to follow a very low-calorie diet. This herb was originally used by African tribes when they would go out on long hunting expeditions and couldn't eat for days at a time.
- L-Carnitine: This helps transport fat cells into the muscles for use as fuel.
- Yohimbe: This enhances blood flow to areas of the body that experience reduced rates of fat burning, improving overall results.

Just like with a pre-workout product, each fat burner is unique so it's important to take some time to consider what the supplement contains and whether it's right for you. If you are using a fat burner, you likely don't need to use a pre-workout product as well because both products are going to give you energy and doubling up may just be a little too much for your body.

Fat burners should always be used with caution as most do stimulate the central nervous system. Start with the lowest recommended dose and then build up from there if you are going to keep using it. And always remember that a fat burner is not going to do the work for you. You still must make sure that you are following a proper nutrition plan along with a workout while on the fat burner. Too many people think that just because they are using a fat burner, they no longer have to watch what they eat.

This isn't true at all. No fat burner will overcome poor nutrition, so look after your nutrition first and then consider a fat burner from there. Remember, although these supplements can give great results, they do come with a set of warnings. Individuals with high blood pressure, heart diseases, thyroid disorders and anxiety issues should not be using these supplements. Whether healthy or with an underlying disorder, always take these burners under the supervision of a certified nutritionist or doctor.

I have tried to simplify the entire text above by compiling a table of all the supplements as per their requirements. This will work as an easy guide for you if and when you decide to supplement:

Supplement	Suggested Dosage (per serving)	Recommended Time of Consumption						Guidelines
		Pre-Workout	During Workout	Post Workout	With a Meal	Empty Stomach	Bedtime	
Macronutrient								
Whey protein	25 grams			✓	✓		✓	A must-have for vegetarians to keep up with protein requirements
Casein	25 grams				✓		✓	Great for keeping the body anabolic before bed (slow-digesting protein)
Hemp protein	25 grams				✓		✓	A great source of omega-3 and protein for vegetarians
Soy protein	25 grams				✓	✓	✓	A rich source of protein for vegetarians

Supplement	Suggested Dosage (per serving)	Recommended Time of Consumption						Guidelines
		Pre-Workout	During Workout	Post Workout	With a Meal	Empty Stomach	Bedtime	
Meal replacement powder	25–50 grams				✓	✓		Great for those looking to gain weight or eat healthy on the go
Waxy maize	30–50 grams			✓				Provides rapid post-exercise recovery
Karbolyn	30–50 grams			✓				Provides rapid post-exercise recovery
Dextrose	25–60 grams			✓				Provides rapid post-exercise recovery
Energy gels	1 gel sachet	✓	✓	✓				Great for improved athletic performance
Sports drinks	250–500 ml	✓	✓	✓				Great for improved athletic performance

Supplement	Suggested Dosage (per serving)	Recommended Time of Consumption						Guidelines
		Pre-Workout	During Workout	Post Workout	With a Meal	Empty Stomach	Bedtime	
Micronutrient								
Calcium	1000 mg					✓	✓	For the lactose intolerant
Magnesium	310 mg (women) 400 mg (men)					✓		Helps boost the immune system
Iron	18 mg (women) 8 mg (men)					✓		Great for improving energy and endurance during exercise
Vitamin D	2000 IU						✓	Great for strong bones

Supplement	Suggested Dosage (per serving)	Recommended Time of Consumption						Guidelines
		Pre-Workout	During Workout	Post Workout	With a Meal	Empty Stomach	Bedtime	
Vitamin C	90 mg (men) 75 mg (women)					✓		Great for immune strength
B Complex vitamins						✓		Great for ongoing energy
Zinc	8 mg (women) 11 mg (men)					✓	✓	Great for hormonal and energy support
Selenium	55 mcg (men) 55 mcg (women)				-		✓	Important for immune and reproductive health
Chromium	25 mg (women) 35 mg (men)						✓	Good for insulin and blood sugar management

Supplement	Suggested Dosage (per serving)	Recommended Time of Consumption						Guidelines
		Pre-Workout	During Workout	Post Workout	With a Meal	Empty Stomach	Bedtime	
Ergogenic								
Creatine Monohydrate	5–10 grams	✓		✓				Important for delaying fatigue and assisting strength and power development
BCAA	4–6 grams	✓	✓	✓				Speeds recovery and improves muscular energy
Caffeine	100–200 mg	✓				✓		Increases alertness, focus and performance, may also enhance fat burning

Supplement	Suggested Dosage (per serving)	Recommended Time of Consumption						Guidelines
		Pre-Workout	During Workout	Post Workout	With a Meal	Empty Stomach	Bedtime	
Ephedrine	8 mg	✓				✓		Increases energy, metabolic rate and performance
Beta-Alanine	3 grams	✓	✓					Can help delay the onset of fatigue during intense exercise
Citrulline Malate or Nitric Oxide	2–4 grams	✓	✓	✓				Great for increasing energy levels
Taurine	500–2000 mg	✓	✓					Can boost mental focus, concentration and stamina

Supplement	Suggested Dosage (per serving)	Recommended Time of Consumption						Guidelines
		Pre-Workout	During Workout	Post Workout	With a Meal	Empty Stomach	Bedtime	
Vitamin B12	2.4–2.6 mcg	✓	✓			✓		Assists with increased energy
Glutamine	5 grams	✓		✓			✓	Speeds recovery and strengthens the immune system
Fat-burning Supplements								
CLA	2–7 grams/day	✓				✓	✓	Great for enhanced metabolic rate, immune system and blood glucose regulation

Supplement	Suggested Dosage (per serving)	Recommended Time of Consumption						Guidelines
		Pre-Workout	During Workout	Post Workout	With a Meal	Empty Stomach	Bedtime	
L-Carnitine	500–2000 mg	✓			✓	✓	✓	Helps transport fatty acids to the muscular cells for energy
Yohimbe	0.2 mg/kg body weight	✓				✓		Can increase blood flow to areas where fat is harder to burn (stubborn fat areas)

Note: The recommended time of consumption doesn't reflect the frequency of dosage. These supplements can be consumed over and above your food intake.

Now that we've finished talking about supplements, let's move forward and understand the various kinds of sports and the key elements of fitness required to play these sports.

PART V

SPORTS TRAINING

An athletic training programme is a mixture of various types of exercises that athletes use for training for each and every day. Their sport-specific training is refined so that they are constantly focusing on getting better and better at various fitness elements.

This section touches upon these vital components of fitness, as well as some of the most commonly performed sports that you can take up, and exercise that one needs to possess to successfully achieve an athletic body.

13

SPORTS TO CONSIDER FOR A FIT AND HEALTHY BODY

Once you've decided that you are going to work towards becoming more athletic in your day-to-day life, you then need to determine which sport it is that you specifically want to pursue.

As we noted earlier, some people will be drawn to a particular type of sport because they have a body type that simply lends well to that form of exercise.

For instance, if you are pure ectomorph—tall, thin and not very muscular or powerful—you are the perfect candidate to become a marathoner. Chances are you also enjoy distance running because you are good at it; it is quite easy for you and you've always loved how it makes your body feel.

On the other hand, if you are a pure endomorph—carrying a good 20 kilograms more, not all that fast and definitely not good at running—becoming a marathoner likely isn't on your to-do list any time soon. In fact, you *hate* running—and that's an understatement. There is nothing drawing you towards the sport, and you're probably considering a comparatively comfortable activity such as racquet sports or swimming.

Finding the right sport to take up is about figuring out what you like and enjoy and what piques your interest, as well as looking at what you would be good at. For almost all people, being good at something they spend a decent amount of time doing is important. Chances are if you are terrible at a particular sport and remain terrible, despite putting in a large amount of effort to try and improve, you won't keep going at it. You'll just end up frustrated and unmotivated. So choosing a sport that interests you and that you are physically capable of improving at, given your body type and training availability, is the key to your success.

This said, let me walk you through some of the most commonly played sports so that you can get a better idea of what they will do for your body and whether you would be a good candidate to start playing them.

Racquet Sports

'I want the same thing I've wanted since I was seven-years-old. I want to be number one.'
Novak Djokovic, Serbian tennis player

Racquet Sports: Tennis, Squash and Badminton

The first lot of sports to consider are racquet sports, namely tennis, squash and badminton. While each of these sports has the same overall objective—to hit an object over a net with a racquet—each one will train your body in a unique way and place different demands on your fitness level.

Tennis

Tennis is a sport that is quite intense in nature, requiring players to be at the peak of their physical condition. To play tennis, you'll need to have a high level of the performance mix, which includes the key elements of fitness that we will discuss in the next chapters.

First, you'll need to develop your agility level. This will help you be fast on your feet and able to constantly switch directions as you receive each pass. In addition, you'll also need to have a high amount of strength and power. You need to drive that ball across the net as quickly as possible, which will, in turn, make it hard for your opponent to hit the ball back over to you. Ever noticed Rafael Nadal's fierce forehand shots? The power he generates outplays his opponents in no time.

Speed is also of the essence when playing tennis. If you lack speed, you won't be fast enough to run across the court to receive a pass sent over to your side, resulting in your opponent gaining a point. Having a high level of endurance in tennis is also key to playing it successfully. If you lack endurance, you'll find that you begin to fatigue in the first part of the game, leaving your performance suffering and your opponent taking over the match.

Tennis is one of the most demanding sports out there and while there is a lot of stop-and-go movement, you need to be able to sustain this movement for an extended period of time to last the match. There isn't a lot of downtime during tennis and so, if you lack this endurance, it will impact your performance in a very negative way.

Finally, you also need to be flexible for this sport, especially at your shoulder girdle and spinal column as this will ensure that you are able to twist and turn to receive the serve over to your side. Very rarely will you find a ball coming directly towards you (it's your opponent's goal to avoid this), and you'll need flexibility to handle this.

Tennis is a great choice of activity if you hope to develop muscular strength as well as dramatically improve your heart health. The stop-and-go nature of tennis, especially while playing at high-intensity levels, makes it very similar to that of a High-Intensity Interval Training session, which is one of the best forms of cardiovascular activity to improve your overall strength conditioning levels.

Playing tennis will also boost heart health, improve circulation, strengthen your bones and help you experience great weight control. You'll burn quite a large amount of energy with each game or training session, and thanks to the nature of the sport, you'll continue to burn energy for hours after the session is completed, which really lends well to optimizing your body composition.

Tennis athletes typically have a body type that will best resemble a mesomorph as they are quite lean and nicely muscled, but at the same time, they aren't overly muscular to the point where they look bulky. This doesn't mean that only natural mesomorphs can play tennis. All body types can train for and participate in tennis and as they do— provided they are training correctly—their body will begin taking on more and more properties of the mesomorph body type.

Squash

Squash is very similar to tennis, with the main difference being that rather than your opponent being across a net from you, they are in the same playing space and both of you are hitting the ball directly against a wall.

Because of the fact that the ball has to travel a shorter distance in squash to be back into play, squash tends to be a very fast-paced game. This means that you'll need to be even quicker on your feet and will have even less downtime to rest and recover.

Squash players need to have a very high level of muscular endurance so that they can sustain play for the duration of the match. Since squash is played on a court that's blocked with four walls around it, the ball will constantly be bouncing back into play, which can cause the rallies to go on much longer than they would in tennis. With tennis, generally speaking, there may only be between two and ten serves across the net before the ball goes out of bounds. With squash, this tends to be much higher thus resulting in a longer playing time and a greater demand on endurance.

When it comes to the strength required, tennis does typically come out ahead in this regard. While squash players will still need to be strong, both the squash racket and the ball used in play are lighter, meaning you don't need to have as much force behind you to hit the ball into play. As the ball also hits the wall in a shorter distance, it reduces the total amount of force you need to hit it with in order to get a good shot in.

As far as flexibility goes, both sports will require you to be constantly reaching and twisting to be able to hit the ball into play. However, a serve in tennis is going to require far more flexibility as well as overall skill as compared to one in squash. Nevertheless, flexibility is important in squash as well. Squash also requires a high level of agility during play as you'll be continually shifting your body around in order to hit the ball and move around the squash court. The two sports are about equal in this regard.

Finally, just as with tennis, speed is of the essence in squash. It is possibly even more important here than in tennis because, in a sense, you have the four walls acting as opponents, hitting the ball back to you. For those who really want to possess a body that's quick, agile, fit and strong, squash is a great game to consider playing.

Badminton

Finally, the last of the racquet sports we'll discuss is badminton, which is quite a bit different from both squash and tennis. With badminton, rather than hitting a ball across the net, you hit a shuttlecock, which is much lighter in weight and will simply float across the net (depending on the type of hit being used by the opponent).

Badminton players will still need a decent amount of endurance as their matches can go on for quite some time, but the overall level of endurance will typically be less than what's needed in both squash and tennis. Badminton players also won't require the same degree of strength as that of squash or tennis players, simply because the racquet and shuttlecock are of much lighter weight. That said, players will require a high degree of speed and quickness.

Badminton courts are typically smaller than tennis courts and the players stand closer to the net, so they can hit the shuttlecock just over the net, resulting in a close-up strike. Players can also use more power and hit the shuttlecock to the back of the court, requiring the opponent to run all the way back in order to receive the shot. This variability will require a high amount of speed, both to be able to react to the serve as well as hit the serve as you intend. Badminton players also need a good level of agility. If they lack agility and fast reflexes, it's highly likely their opponent will be able to overtake them during the match.

Those who play badminton tend to be less muscular overall than those who play squash or tennis, so it's a great sport for ectomorphs to venture into. However, mesomorphs or endomorphs should not be turned off because if they can gain the level of speed needed for badminton, they too can excel at this sport.

Badminton is a great way to develop your overall cardiovascular fitness levels, assist with weight management and promote body composition improvements. Like tennis and squash, badminton also has that stop-and-go feature to it, which will help to ramp up your metabolic rate for hours after training or playing, mimicking the effect of an interval cardio training session.

Regardless of which racquet sport you choose to play, you can expect to make great improvements in your speed and agility as well as your cardiovascular fitness levels. You may also experience great improvements in your strength and power as well if you choose to play either squash or tennis.

Swimming

'I feel most at home in the water. I disappear.
That's where I belong.'
Michael Phelps, American Olympic swimmer

Swimming

Another sport that you might consider engaging in, to help achieve a higher level of fitness and become more like an athlete, is swimming. Swimming is a very good option for anyone who tends to suffer from joint aches and pains (or full-blown arthritis) as it is non-impact in nature, and your joints will be resting easy while you perform.

Swimming requires full body strength as both your legs and arms are moving constantly to help propel you forward. Your core, that is your abdominal muscles, is also used as it contracts to keep you moving through the water as quickly as possible. Swimmers tend to have very nicely muscled upper bodies, especially in and around the shoulder region, as these muscles are employed with each stroke. As such, these athletes will need to focus on strength training for the shoulder. Unfortunately, some of the smaller rotator cuff muscles can be injured very quickly if one is not careful in this sport.

Depending on the type of swimming one does, you also need to possess good amounts of endurance as well. This endurance may be longer duration endurance or it may be a much shorter level of endurance if doing a short-distance race. However you choose to look at it, swimmers will need to a have some degree of muscular endurance. Additionally, the shorter the duration of the race or the distance one is swimming, the more strength will be required. So in those instances, it becomes more about strength endurance than just flat out cardiovascular endurance.

Swimmers will also want to possess some degree of agility but because they are not moving around on their feet, the requirement won't be nearly as great as for those doing sports that involve running. Nevertheless, when a swimmer reaches one end of the pool and needs to turn around to swim the other direction, executing this movement flawlessly will still require a good amount of agility.

Flexibility is another element of the performance mix, which is very important to be a truly great swimmer. The athlete must be flexible at the shoulder joints so that they can execute all the swimming strokes properly and easily. If they are inflexible, it may make it harder for them to develop the strength and power they otherwise would have when performing a particular stroke.

So overall, swimmers are athletes who possess a great level of athleticism across all spectrums of the performance mix. Swimmers will typically train both in the water as well as out of the water to ensure that they are developing these characteristics and preparing themselves the best they can for any races or events they may choose to take part in. In terms of functional fitness, swimming will increase everyday muscular strength to some degree, making it easier to perform normal lifestyle activities and boost cardiovascular endurance, which will help ensure you aren't left feeling winded as you go about your daily lifestyle.

Swimmers tend to develop body types that are between the ectomorph and mesomorph and they will also possess a good amount of muscle. However, too much bulk is not desirable because it can make it harder to get through the water by creating additional resistance for the athlete.

As swimming greatly utilizes both the upper as well as the lower body, this makes it a terrific option as far as calorie burning goes. Swimming is a good option for anyone who is hoping to achieve excellent body weight control. The one caveat, though: If you do choose to take part in swimming, beware of your appetite. Being in cold water does tend to make

most people hungry. If you come out of each swim only to eat
large volumes of food, it could have negative implications for
your body weight. Provided you are mindful of this, swimming
is an excellent way to achieve an optimal body weight and
body composition.

Running

'I try to lead by example.'

Usain Bolt, Jamaican sprinter

Marathon Running

The next sport we will discuss is marathon running. If you stop and picture a marathoner, what comes to your mind? Chances are you're envisioning someone who's lean, tall and rather lanky looking. They don't have much muscle and may appear to be all 'lungs and legs', which is how marathoners are often described.

While you will find that marathoners can come in all different shapes and sizes, as more and more people set out to achieve running a marathon as their own personal goal, the truly great marathoners are those that tend to have a relatively low body weight as this allows them to more easily transport themselves over long distances.

Think about it this way: If you had to run for three or more hours, would you want to do it with a backpack full of books strapped to your back? Clearly not, which illustrates why it's much better to be lighter for this sport. As flat ground running, which is what most marathon running is, doesn't require a whole lot of muscular power, it simply doesn't make sense to have much muscle bulk. Marathoners just don't need a high level of strength and the extra weight will only hinder them.

So marathoners tend to be quite low in the strength department, but they are the epitome of endurance. No other sport requires the level of endurance that running a marathon does, and this is where marathoners really shine. If great cardiovascular health is your goal, marathon running can provide it.

In the flexibility department, marathoners should possess a relatively good degree of flexibility when this will ensure that they can achieve proper strides when they run.

If they are very stiff and tight, it could shorten their stride, which means more strides per given distance must be taken, which in turn burns up precious energy they are likely trying to conserve.

Speed is something that most marathoners won't need to worry about because when it comes to running, the greater the distance of a race, the slower the pace. And since nothing is longer than a marathon (except perhaps an ultra-marathon, which falls in the same category), 'fast' is not a word you would use to describe these runners.

Despite this, if an athlete is looking to become the best in their class, they will have to do some speed work at being fast to get ahead of their opponents. But mostly, if you are trying to achieve an athletic lifestyle, initially you would have the goal of finishing the race in which case, speed isn't important. But over time, you will begin to require speed because at some stage you will want to fight your personal best.

Finally, agility is something that marathoners must possess to a slight degree as well. This is more for when high levels of fatigue set in after they have been running for hours and they start to feel quite wobbly on their legs. If you've ever watched a marathon event and seen runners collapse upon crossing the finishing line, you have an idea of just how shaky those last steps can be. Fatigue is at an all-time high and it's everything they can do to just stay on their feet. If they have no agility whatsoever, it can make it quite challenging to do so.

Making the decision to become a marathoner is not a decision to take lightly as the demands on your body, as well as on your time and schedule, will be great. That said, it's a good sport to get into if you like a lot of alone time when exercising, want to build up great cardiovascular fitness levels, lose some weight, love to eat (because you will be eating A LOT closer to marathon events!) and are all about excelling your personal bests.

Cycling

'Pain is temporary. Quitting lasts forever.'

Lance Armstrong, American cyclist

Cycling

Cycling is one of the best sports to consider when you make the decision to achieve an athletic lifestyle. Cycling is a non-impact sport, unlike running a marathon. Non-impact sports basically don't add an additional load on your joints, especially the knee joints. While in some cases it may be hard on the knees if you are cycling against a path of great resistance, most people will simply not have a problem.

Cycling needs good cardiovascular endurance as it does require you to continue on at a fixed pace for a period of time. Here again, you can participate in long cycling events, requiring greater muscular endurance, or you can participate in shorter cycling events, which will require some endurance but a much greater degree of overall muscular strength. The nature of your event will determine just how much time you need to spend in endurance-related training.

Strength is the next element of the performance mix to consider and is one that cyclists must possess, especially when it comes to their lower body strength levels. As you will almost always be pedalling against some degree of resistance, this will, over time, build up the lower body muscles. Typically, cyclists are also expected to do ongoing strength training workouts for their lower body in order to build more muscular power and strength. The stronger a cyclist is in their lower body, the easier it will be to travel the distance that they need to cover.

Think of your leg power in direct correlation to the level of engine power you have in your car. The more powerful your car's engine, the faster it will go. It is the same for you on your bike. If you can build up the strongest engine possible (your legs), this will come in very handy when it comes to being the fastest cyclist you can be.

One thing that cyclists won't need to have is a high amount of flexibility because this is one sport that doesn't require too great a range of motion, such that even those who are relatively inflexible can still pedal a bike just fine. That said, don't think that adding in some flexibility training is not important. Flexibility is still critical to success since it will help with injury prevention. One thing cyclists will notice is that after an intense session of cycling, their quad and hamstring muscles may get very tight and tense. If these muscles are not stretched out, the pain may linger, leaving them sore and making it harder to train again sooner. Regular flexibility training will help relieve this soreness, and should be included as part of a regular cycling routine.

Speed is the next performance mix factor to consider and is one that cyclists will want to be quite strong in as well. The greater the speed of the cyclist, the faster they will be able to pedal ahead to the finish, which is the objective of cycling races.

Finally, a fair amount of agility is also required for cycling just to maintain your position on the bike itself. If a cyclist lacks basic agility, they'll find themselves falling off the bike easily, which will make it near impossible to complete a race. Most people will be able to obtain this basic level of agility, however, do keep in mind that the greater the fatigue is, the harder it will be to stay on the bike. Similarly, if you are doing sprint cycling events, you may be adopting severe leans towards the curve as you round corners, which will require a high degree of agility as well.

Cycling is a great alternative endurance sport for those who dislike running and serves to increase both cardiovascular fitness as well as muscular strength. Best of all, given its low impact, it's typically easier on the athlete's body than other sports are.

Cricket

'I just keep it simple.
Watch the ball and play it on merit.'
Sachin Tendulkar, Indian cricketer

Cricket

Finally, the last sport you may choose to participate in, if you are someone who tends to be more interested in group fitness activities, is cricket. Cricket is played in a team, so each team member is responsible for his or her own role in the sport. Each of these positions will put different elements of your fitness to the test.

For instance, the batsman will need to have a high amount of both strength and speed, as he'll be responsible for hitting the ball into play. If he's lacking in either one attribute, the ball won't go nearly as far, which will make it easier for the opposing team to take him out of the game. After the ball is hit, the batsman must then begin running, and will require a mix of speed and endurance to execute his position.

The bowler must possess a high level of strength and endurance as he'll be delivering the ball multiple times through the game and focusing on delivering it as fast as possible to the batsman. The faster he delivers it, the harder it will be to hit and the greater the chances he bowls the batsman out.

Catchers in the field are going to require a high degree of agility and speed as they must focus and balance themselves to catch the ball and in doing so, be prepared to change directions very rapidly. The faster they can do this, the more successfully they will contribute to their team's chance of success.

Each of the players on a cricket team thoroughly knows their roles and this helps them understand how to best modify their training to be at the top of their game. A bowler will spend far more time developing his strength and power as compared to a batsman, who will need to spend more time on power and speed work.

Choosing to participate in cricket is a great idea if you are a team player. Cricket is not only a high-spirited sport but also includes a lot of variety. The game of cricket is constantly changing and no two games will ever be alike, as opposed to marathon running, for instance, where each time you head out for a training session, you can virtually expect the same type of activity to repeat over and over again, with the exception of varying running paths, distances and speed.

So there you have a closer look at some of the most commonly played sports to consider as you begin your journey of becoming an athlete.

Let's now try and understand a few terms we have just come across, which are the key elements of athletic training, in a little more detail.

14

KEY PHYSICAL ELEMENTS OF SPORTS TRAINING

In order to become great at a sport, there are a number of physical characteristics that you must possess. An athlete will have certain levels of these characteristics, all of which come together to contribute to their overall performance level. Some athletes may possess more of one element than others, as required by their chosen sport, but to some degree they will possess all the elements.

Let's identify what these elements are so that you can understand how they fit into the picture of becoming an athlete.

Strength

The very first element athletes need to possess is strength. A strong athlete is one who is able to generate a large amount of force through their muscular contractions in order to achieve a particular goal. When we speak of strength here, we are not referring to, in general terms, how fast an athlete can move. In the context of sports, speed is something else entirely, which we will talk about momentarily.

Strength here means sheer force. It is typically improved through resistance-based exercises, such as weightlifting, body weight training, utilizing resistance bands or some other external resistance medium. Possessing a good level of strength is not only important for maximum performance but also for injury prevention. The stronger one's muscles are, the less likely one is to get injured.

Finally, keeping your strength levels up is one of the most important things to do if you hope to sustain a high quality of life. Those who don't regularly do some form of strength-training activities will slowly but surely start to see their strength level declining, leading to muscle mass loss. If your body is no longer forced to put its strength to use, the body will see no reason to keep it.

For ageing individuals, this is a very serious concern. Loss of strength may not seem too severe at first if you are no longer engaging in athletic events. But when your loss of strength starts making it hard for you to carry groceries from the car or move a relatively heavy object in your home, it becomes frustrating. If you begin to rely on other people to help you do the most basic tasks, which may happen as you reach your sixties and seventies, your quality of life will be very low. For some of you reading this right now, your sixties and seventies are still quite far way, but know that strength is something you want to keep up to ensure a high quality of life now and in the future.

The good news is that for functional everyday strength, you don't need to do much to maintain or advance your strength levels. A few strength training sessions per week, lasting around twenty to thirty minutes each, is more than sufficient. Of course, if your goal is to improve athletic strength, you'll want to devote more time than this to it, but it is one area of your physical fitness that you can maintain or improve on without having to devote hours each week to it.

Endurance

The next element of athleticism that most athletes develop to one degree or another is endurance. Endurance refers to how long one can sustain a given level of force for. Depending on the sport, this level may vary quite a lot. For instance, the endurance level of a marathoner, who sustains very little force, will be very long in duration. Compare this to the endurance level of a sprinter, who maintains great force but only for a very short duration. While both athletes need some degree of endurance to sustain their desired force, the marathoner requires a much longer-lasting level of endurance as compared to the sprinter.

The only athletes who don't need to sustain ongoing endurance are the ones utilizing max-out effort, or in other words, using all their strength and power to get that ace shot, say, for example, a powerlifter or a javelin thrower. If they plan on repeating these actions (after a rest period has elapsed), they will still need some degree of endurance to do so. This is called intermittent endurance and it refers to the capability of performing maximum intensity exercise over and over again. If they are fatigued after just one try, as you might imagine they could be, it would make it very challenging to perform training sessions and see improvement.

Maintaining a good level of endurance is not just important in the athletic realm but in daily life as well. Those who are lacking in endurance will fatigue very quickly when doing daily tasks and this can really hamper their quality of life. Endurance is one characteristic that can be lost quite quickly when it's not being trained for, so it requires effort to keep up. While you won't lose endurance if you take three to four days off, for instance, if you go a week without training for it, you may start to notice some decrements.

Many athletes who train for endurance will notice that if they take a week off, when they come back, they aren't quite as good as they were before. Fortunately, they will regain their endurance quickly with regular training, but it's important to note that this is one factor you need to constantly keep working towards.

Speed and Power

The next element that needs to be in place is speed. Speed refers to how fast an athlete can carry out a given pattern of movement. Some athletes need to be very speedy, such as a sprinter, while other athletes don't need to concern themselves as much with speed, such as the marathoner for whom endurance is the bigger factor. Still though, if the marathoner lacks speed entirely, they will never win the race as there will be others who are simply faster when the time comes. Speed is relative to the event that is being performed, but in most athletic events, speed does come into play in determining optimal performance.

In relation to speed, you also have power. Speed and power are slightly different, despite the fact that many people do attempt to use the terms interchangeably. While speed simply refers to how fast someone is doing something, power refers to how fast they are while carrying out a certain level of force. For instance, if you were to just run as fast as you can across a field, you may obtain great speed. However, if you were to pull a weighted object behind you while running across the field, you are demonstrating great power. Power involves a higher degree of sheer strength than speed does. Power combines speed with strength, forming one very powerful athletic trait.

Powerful athletes will be able to move higher loads very quickly and over a distance. Developing this skill takes a long time, dedicated to not only strength-training activities but to speed work as well. When you have excelled at both strength and speed levels, you will develop great power as a result.

Agility

Picture yourself in a square room. You need to sprint and touch each corner of the room, but which corner you need to run to will be decided by someone else. While you are trying to touch every corner, there is a loud command to change direction. You turn yourself to sprint towards that side and there again is a loud command to change direction. Imagine doing this multiple times. If you can do this successfully and quickly, you possess great agility. If you cannot, it's a skill you need to work on.

Agility is yet another important factor involved in the athletic performance mix and refers to how well you know your body in a given space. Basically, agility implies how balanced and quick you are while moving around. Those who lack agility will often find they have trouble 'finding their legs' when doing athletic events or may fall over easily if they are playing a contact sport.

Being agile is important as it will help ensure that you aren't easily thrown off-track by any sort of opposing force that comes your way. It doesn't matter if it is an external opposing force or an internal one, which can happen, for instance, if you try to change directions quickly and don't have iron control over your muscular contractions. You can train for agility by using any sort of training technique that puts the body off-balance and requires you to sustain your position despite this.

Don't overlook how agility impacts you in day-to-day life as well. Those who lack agility will find it harder to do everyday tasks, whether it is walking upstairs, walking across unstable surfaces or performing routine tasks such as cooking and cleaning. Agility impacts almost everything that you do and the less agile you are, the harder you will find it is to move through everyday life.

Flexibility

The last factor that needs to be taken into account is flexibility. This is another important characteristic and is far too often overlooked by athletes because they don't see the direct benefit of training for it. But make no mistake about it, there are big advantages to training for flexibility.

Firstly, flexibility can help improve your performance, both at your sport as well as at other exercises you are doing to improve your performance. For instance, if you are inflexible, you'll have a very hard time performing any sort of weightlifting that requires squatting. Whether it is front squats or back squats, you may not be able to lower your body properly as you simply aren't that flexible. If this is the case, you'll miss out on reaping all the strength gains that squats provide, which would then be transferred over to the level of athletic performance you exhibit.

Similarly, if you are inflexible and are playing tennis, you may not be able to twist your body effectively enough to make a hit that isn't aimed directly at you. You'll miss the hit and your overall performance won't be as great. Hence, flexibility can impact you in a couple of ways, which is why it's something that needs to be worked on. While improving your flexibility doesn't seem as glamorous or exciting like improving your strength or speed does, it is important nevertheless.

Being more flexible is also important for reducing your risk of injury. If you are very inflexible, it's more likely that an opposing force that acts against you, causing you to twist in an unnatural position, will cause a muscle tear or strain, simply because your muscles do not naturally move that far.

Flexibility is also something that must be tended to on a very regular basis, which is why many athletes fail to really see improvements in this regard. If you aren't working on your flexibility daily, you can expect for it to decline.

While athletes can maintain strength and power for quite some time even if they aren't training for it every day, flexibility is fast to decline. In fact, those who don't train for it at all will find themselves quickly growing very tight as they get older and soon, it will be more challenging for them to even do everyday activities they used to enjoy.

The good news, however, is that it doesn't really take all that much to improve or sustain your flexibility. All you really need is to devote ten to fifteen minutes per day after your warm-up. Never attempt to work on this element of your fitness when your muscles are cold because they'll be tense and tight and will not move very far at all. It's always best if you can finish off your training sessions with a few minutes of flexibility work. This will not only help you improve this element of your fitness level, but will also help you cool down.

So there you have a much better look at the main areas of your fitness that you should focus on developing as best as possible. Depending on the sport, you may choose to put far more emphasis on one of these areas as compared to the others, but just remember that all should be tended to in some degree.

Now that we've finished talking about the various sports and the key elements of fitness, let's move forward and put the whole puzzle together. Get ready to eat, train and live like an athlete.

PART VI

LIVE, EAT AND COOK LIKE AN ATHLETE

You may be wondering that with so much time devoted to training, when does an athlete actually manage to eat? And when they eat, what do they eat? Are their shelves full of powders and pills, or do they eat right to get an edge over their performance?

Let's take a closer look and understand what's required to eat like an athlete, so that you can put your plan for an athletic lifestyle into action and get started immediately. In order to begin your journey to eating and training like an athlete, you need to get your kitchen ready to go—just like an athlete.

15

AN ATHLETE'S KITCHEN

The first step in forming an athlete's kitchen is to toss out all the foods that you know you shouldn't be eating. Now, this may be hard for some of you as we do tend to develop a psychological connection with the foods that we enjoy, but if you really want to succeed with your goals, this is essential for you to do. If it's gone from the freezer, fridge and cupboards, there will be a much lower chance of your consuming foods you shouldn't be eating.

As the saying goes, 'out of sight, out of mind'! What should you be tossing? Keep in mind that the list below is by no means exhaustive, but it should give you a pretty good idea of what types of foods need to get the boot from your home:

- Cakes, biscuits, cookies, pastries and other unhealthy baked goods
- Processed meats (sausages, hot dogs)
- Any type of sugary candy (hard candies, chewy candies)
- Fried snacks
- Wannabe diet snacks
- Creamy condiments or sauces
- Salty sauces

- Soft drinks
- Alcohol

If you can remove these items from your kitchen, you will have an excellent head start on eating properly. What you should be stocking your kitchen with is listed in the table below:

Smart Carbs	Quality Proteins	Healthy Fats
Sweet potato or yams	Chicken breast	Peanut butter or almond butter
Brown rice	Turkey breast	Unsalted nuts
Bajra	Seafood (shrimp, crab, lobster, scallops)	Flaxseeds
Rajgira	Low-fat or sugar-free plain yogurt (curd)	Sunflower seeds

Barley	Low-fat paneer	Chia seeds
Oatmeal (unsweetened)	Low-fat milk	Olive oil
Beans	Whey protein powder	Coconut oil
Pulses	Whole eggs or egg whites	Flaxseed oil
Lentils	Soybeans	Avocado oil
Fresh fruit (all varieties)	Tofu	Avocado
Fresh vegetables (all varieties)		

Now that you have your list of preferred foods, let's look at the supplements that will give you an edge performing these sports.

Which Supplement Is Best for Your Sport?

The table below looks at the supplements you should consider for some common sports.

Sport	Supplements
Marathon running	Whey protein powder Carbohydrate gel Carbohydrate powder Sports drinks Caffeine BCAAs Glutamine Vitamin B12

Cycling	Whey protein powder Carbohydrate gel Carbohydrate powder Sports drinks Caffeine BCAAs Glutamine Creatine (for short-duration cycling sprints) Vitamin B12
Tennis, squash or badminton	Whey protein powder Carbohydrate gel Carbohydrate powder Sports drinks Caffeine BCAAs Glutamine Creatine Citrulline malate Beta-Alanine Taurine Vitamin B12
Cricket	Whey protein powder Caffeine Tyrosine BCAAs Glutamine Taurine Vitamin B12

Swimming	Whey protein powder
	Sports drinks
	Caffeine
	BCAAs
	Glutamine
	Creatine
	Citrulline malate
	Beta-Alanine
	Taurine
	Vitamin B12

Keep in mind that you that by no means do you absolutely need to use these supplements; they are simply recommendations if you want to take your training up a notch. But if you do find the need to, you can use any one or a combination of them to complement your training.

Now that we've discussed the various foods in and on the shelf of an athlete, let's look at a few additional considerations that athletes should take into account.

16

EATING LIKE AN ATHLETE

When you chuck these foods out of your life, are you ready to see what your new menu will look like? Putting together a healthy eating plan for yourself takes some time and effort, but it will be well worth it. For starters, you will have higher energy levels, you'll be able to stay focused and concentrate more throughout the day, you'll find that you feel stronger and livelier and you'll notice you sleep better as well. Nutrition really can impact just about every element of your overall well-being, so it's not something to take lightly.

Before I give you a full meal plan to follow, let's first discuss two more considerations: meal frequency and meal composition.

Meal Frequency

One thing to consider, after you have figured out what foods you need to be eating, is how often you should be eating throughout the day. Meal frequency is an important consideration as it dictates how you feel during the day and whether your body has the nutrients it needs as it goes about its day-to-day activities.

While most people typically follow three square meals a day (plus a snack or two), as an athlete, you have greater fuel demands and this isn't going to work for you. You need something that ensures you get your needs met better and more effectively. As such, your meal frequency should increase. Most athletes should be striving to eat five or six meals a day, plus throwing in a post-workout meal or protein shake as well.

And note that these are all meals, not just small snacks. By a meal I mean that each time you eat, you should be getting in some protein along with some carbs and/or fats. An apple as a meal just won't cut it; you need something that is going to sustain you and nourish your body. At first, this might seem like a lot and you might be wondering, 'How could I ever eat six meals a day?' But it's not as hard as you might think.

Once you get going with this pattern, you'll find that your body adapts quickly and soon, you'll naturally want to eat at these times. Plus, as you start to increase your overall activity levels, you'll find your body demanding more fuel and you'll feel the need to eat more often as well. You should ideally aim to schedule your meals evenly throughout the day, eating every three to four hours. This will help ensure that your body constantly has something in its system to digest and use for energy and that you're never running on an empty tank.

These meals may not be as big as you would have eaten if you were just eating three square meals a day. However, these meals will be larger than a traditional snack because your overall energy needs are higher. You can adjust the meal frequency to whatever best suits your routine. Some people will do better using a five meal per day protocol, while others may prefer eating seven or more times.

If you are training for marathons and plan on doing a three-hour run on a particular day, it's likely you'll be eating very often throughout that day. If you have a calorie intake of more than 4000 calories to get in that day, it's much easier to eat eight meals of around 500 calories each than it is to stomach eating four meals at 1000 calories per meal. Eating too large a meal will just lead to feeling lethargic and not feeling like exercising at all. An even distribution is a far wiser approach.

Meal Composition

This brings us to the next point that needs to be considered: meal composition. This basically means *what* each meal is made up of. As you have different needs throughout the day, your meals will have to focus on certain things more than others at different times. Let's look at the main times that you should be considering here:

Pre-Workout

You must be fully aware of your meal composition immediately before any training sessions. If you are eating within sixty to ninety minutes prior to training, keep this meal lower in total fat content, focusing almost exclusively on protein and carbohydrates. Fat takes a longer time to break down and digest in the body and as a result, eating fats before you are going to exercise could leave you feeling rather sluggish and possibly with cramps.

If you are eating more than ninety minutes before working out, you will have more time to digest the meal. A balanced mix of protein, carbohydrates and dietary fats can then be consumed.

Post Workout

This is another time to be careful of what you are eating. Immediately after your workout, focus strictly on protein and carbohydrates. Here again, fat simply digests too slowly and at this time, your primary goal is to get those nutrients to the muscle tissues as rapidly as you possibly can. Fat will only halt this progress, working directly against your goals. Your post-workout meal should focus on fast-acting protein as well as some faster-acting carbohydrates as we discussed in the nutrition section. Save your fat intake for other times during the day.

Breakfast

One time of the day when you will want to add fat to your diet is at breakfast. As breakfast is the meal to kick-start your day with, you don't want to go too light here. Your breakfast meal should contain protein, carbohydrates and dietary fats—and a good dose of each. Skimping on breakfast could leave you feeling far less than energized as your day gets going and this will just lead to a total lack of energy as the afternoon comes along.

The last thing you want to be doing is playing catch-up with your energy levels. By starting your day off with a hearty breakfast, you won't have to. It's often said that for optimal energy levels breakfast should be the largest meal of the day, with each subsequent meal becoming smaller and smaller.

This is generally a good principle to follow but for athletic training, the meals following workouts will typically be as big, if not bigger, than breakfast, as this is the time when your body is most in need of nourishment to help replenish the energy used during exercise.

Before Bed

Another time to be mindful of meal composition is right before bed. The last thing you want to do before bed is eat a very heavy meal, as this could cause you to lie awake in bed at night digesting your food and not sleeping. You also don't want to eat too many simple carbohydrates prior to bedtime as this could lead to an increase in blood sugar followed by a crash shortly after, causing you to wake up hungry during the night.

Instead, focus on a light snack before bed, containing protein along with some healthy fats. A few complex carbs can be added if you wish, but try and keep those lower and stick to a high fibre meal. The only exception to this is if you are performing a late-night training session. In this case, you want to eat a meal rich in carbohydrates as your desire to get adequate recovery nutrition should trump the fact that you will be going to bed shortly.

Apart from these times, focus on well-balanced meals during the rest of the day. Most athletes should eat a mixed diet consisting of around 25–30 per cent protein, 50–60 per cent carbohydrates and 20–35 per cent dietary fat. Adjust nutrients to figure out what ratio you feel best using and then form your diet plan from there.

With the basic knowledge of sports nutrition and how to pick a sport to play, let's carry on and see what a weekly schedule might look like for a person undertaking athletic training and a complementing, sport-specific nutrition plan.

17

A PEEK INTO YOUR WEEKLY TRAINING SCHEDULE

Wondering how this all fits together? What does the training and eating plan to become a good athlete look like? Let me show you a sample monthly schedule for an athlete participating in each of the sports that we've discussed in this book, namely marathon running, cycling, racquet sports and cricket.

The monthly exercise schedules below illustrate when you might perform your sport-specific training as well as the types of exercise you would do in the gym to improve these efforts. Keep in mind that these are very generalized programmes and are intended for informational purposes only. If you are planning on taking part in any of these sports, it's best to seek assistance from a trainer or coach of that sport along with a sports nutritionist. They will be best able to assess your overall skill level as well as your current fitness capacity and generate a training and nutrition plan that's right for you. A good sports training programme will always be tailored to the athlete in question as this will be what best helps them progress forward. For a full explanation of the exercises that I have recommended, please refer to the glossary at the end of the book.

After the training schedule, you'll also find a sample daily eating schedule for both your training as well as rest days during the week. Keep in mind the amounts you eat will vary based on your own body weight and daily activity level. However, this should give you a pretty good idea of the types of food and meal plan layouts that you should emulate.

Let's look at each sport now individually.

Racquet Sports
Four Week Workout Plan

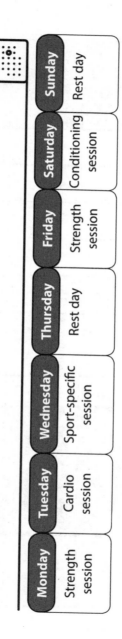

Monday	Tuesday	Wednesday	Thursday	Friday	Saturday	Sunday
Strength session	Cardio session	Sport-specific session	Rest day	Strength session	Conditioning session	Rest day

The tables below provide a broad idea of what each workout session should look like:

Strength Session Workout Plan: The strength training protocols may continue for up to twelve weeks.

Excercise Order	Exercise	Sets	Rest Pertiod	Repetitions					Duration
				Set 1	Set 2	Set 3	Set 4	Set 5	
1	Warm-up: Treadmill or elliptical machine or rowing or cycling								10 minutes
2	Back squats: Start with two light warm-up sets	5	2 minutes	15	12	10	6	3	Maximum 60 seconds per set
3	Start with two light warm-up sets of bench press, followed by a superset								

Exercise Order	Exercise	Sets	Rest Period	Set 1	Set 2	Set 3	Set 4	Set 5	Duration
	Superset: Flat bench press with lat pulldown								
	Barbell bench press	3	60 seconds	10	8	6			Maximum 60 seconds per set
	Lat pulldown	3		10	8	6			Maximum 60 seconds per set
4	**Super set: Shoulder press with rotator cuff**								
	Seated dumb-bell shoulder press	4	60 seconds	12	10	8	6		Maximum 60 seconds per set
	Rotator cuff external rotation	4		15	15	15	15		Maximum 60 seconds per set
5	TheraBand raises: lateral, front and rear shoulder raises	3	Non-stop	10	10	10			Maximum 60 seconds per set
6	Oblique twists (per side)	4	Non-stop	15	12	10	8		Maximum 60 seconds per set
7	Cool down: Stretches								5 minutes

Note: Increase weights as each set progresses and progressively overload each week by adding 2.5–5 pounds of resistance.

Cardio Session Workout Plan: This is a supplementary workout in order to improve your heart rate for when you're actually playing the sport.

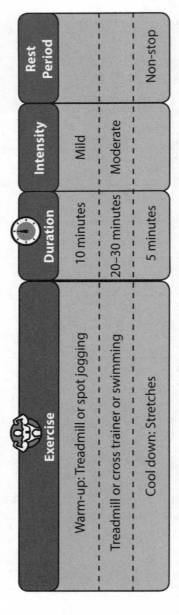

Exercise	Duration	Intensity	Rest Period
Warm-up: Treadmill or spot jogging	10 minutes	Mild	
Treadmill or cross trainer or swimming	20–30 minutes	Moderate	
Cool down: Stretches	5 minutes		Non-stop

Note: Perform this session at an intensity level of around five to six on a scale of one to ten, with ten being maximum effort.

Conditioning Session Workout Plan: The conditioning session will help prevent injuries and boost your ability to exercise at higher intensities for a longer period of time.

Excercise Order	Exercise	Sets	Rest Pertiod	Repetitions					Duration
				Set 1	Set 2	Set 3	Set 4	Set 5	
1	Warm-up: Treadmill or elliptical machine or rowing or cycling								5 minutes
2	Box jumps	5	10 seconds	20	20	15	15	15	Maximum 60 seconds per set
3	Sprints	2	30 seconds						Maximum 60 seconds per set
4	Kettlebell swings	2	10 seconds	20	20				Maximum 60 seconds per set
5	HIIT stationary bike		Non-stop						10 minutes
6	Cool down: Stretches								5 minutes

Sports Session Workout Plan: This session is the reason you are doing other workouts and following a specific nutrition plan. Enjoy this day.

Exercise Order	Exercise	Duration	Intensity	Rest Period
1	Warm-up: Spot jog or neck and shoulder rotations or free shots	10 minutes	Mild	
2	A game of squash/tennis/badminton	As per game duration	High intensity	As per game duration
3	Cool down: Stretches	5 minutes	Mild	

Note: Have fun. Play your best game.

Meal Plans

The exact time of all your meals will depend upon your daily schedule and the time of day you plan to train. The pre-workout snacks can be consumed anywhere between one to three hours before training begins. There should be enough time for your stomach to feel comfortable—not too full and not too hungry. The time of the pre-workout snack will, however, depend upon how efficiently you will digest the food. The post-workout meals should ideally be consumed immediately after your workout in order to start the process of refuelling.

Workout Day Meal Plan

Meal 1	Pre-workout	Post Workout	Meal 4	Meal 5
1 cup oats	1 vegetable sandwich	1 banana	100 grams chicken breast or 150 grams tofu	1 tablespoon peanut butter
2 whole eggs scrambled with 1 cup diced vegetables	100 grams chicken breast or paneer	2 scoops whey isolate protein powder	1 cup cooked brown rice	1 cup skimmed milk
1 orange	1 banana	1 scoop BCAAs (you can sip this during the session as well)	1 cup steamed vegetables	5–6 black raisins
1 cup skimmed milk				

Non-Workout Day Meal Plan

Meal 1	Meal 2	Meal 3	Meal 4	Meal 5
½ cup oats	1 medium-sized sweet potato	15 almonds	5–6 egg whites	100 grams chicken breast
2 whole eggs scrambled with 1 cup diced vegetables	100 grams grilled fish	½ cup paneer	1 cup salad greens with 1 tablespoon olive oil based salad dressing	1 small bajra or jowar or whole wheat chapatti
½ orange	1 cup steamed vegetables	1 cup pomegranate	½ cup brown rice	¼ sliced avocado
				Diced peppers, cucumbers, mushrooms

Cycling
Four Week Workout Plan

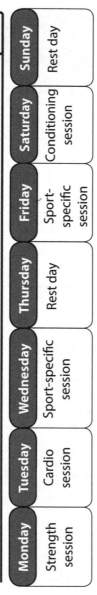

Monday	Tuesday	Wednesday	Thursday	Friday	Saturday	Sunday
Strength session	Cardio session	Sport-specific session	Rest day	Sport-specific session	Conditioning session	Rest day

The tables below provide a broad idea of what each workout session should look like:

Strength Session Workout Plan: The strength training protocols may continue for up to twelve weeks.

Exercise Order	Exercise	Sets	Rest Period	Repetitions					Duration
				Set 1	Set 2	Set 3	Set 4	Set 5	
1	Warm-up: Treadmill or elliptical machine or rowing or cycling								10 minutes
2	Back squats: Start with two light warm-up sets	5	2 minutes	15	12	10	6	3	Maximum 60 seconds per set
3	Sumo deadlifts: Two light warm-up sets	3	2 minutes	10	8	6			Maximum 60 seconds per set

Excercise Order	Exercise	Sets	Rest Pertiod	Repetitions					Duration
				Set 1	Set 2	Set 3	Set 4	Set 5	
4	Power cleans with standing calf raises	4	2 minutes	12	10	8	6		Maximum 60 seconds per set
5	TheraBand raises: lateral, front and rear shoulder raises	3	Non-stop	10	10	10			Maximum 60 seconds per set
6	Walking lunges: Two light warm-up sets	4	60 seconds	12	10	8	6		Maximum 60 seconds per set
7	Cool down: Stretches								10 minutes

Note: Increase weights as each set progresses and progressively overload each week by adding 2.5–5 pounds of resistance.

Cardio Session Workout Plan: This is a supplementary workout in order to improve your heart rate for when you're actually playing the sport.

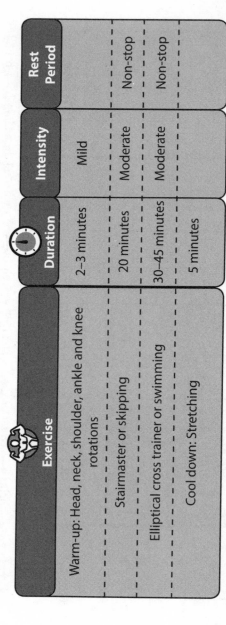

Exercise	Duration	Intensity	Rest Period
Warm-up: Head, neck, shoulder, ankle and knee rotations	2–3 minutes	Mild	
Stairmaster or skipping	20 minutes	Moderate	Non-stop
Elliptical cross trainer or swimming	30–45 minutes	Moderate	Non-stop
Cool down: Stretching	5 minutes		

Note: Perform this session at an intensity level of around six to seven on a scale of one to ten, with ten being maximum effort.

Conditioning Session Workout Plan: The conditioning session will help boost your ability to exercise at higher intensities for a longer period of time.

Exercise Order	Exercise	Sets	Rest Period	Repetitions					Duration
				Set 1	Set 2	Set 3	Set 4	Set 5	
1	Warm-up: Treadmill or elliptical machine or rowing or cycling								5 minutes
2	Sprints	5	30 seconds						60 seconds between sets
3	Kettlebell clean and press	5	60 seconds	20	20	15	15	15	60 seconds per set
4	HIIT stationary bike		Non-stop						30 minutes
5	Cool down: Stretches								5 minutes

Note: Maintain focus during this workout.

Sports Session Workout Plan: This session is the reason you are doing other workouts and following a specific nutrition plan. Enjoy this day.

Exercise Order	Exercise	Duration	Intensity	Rest Period
1	Warm-up: Spot jogging or all joint rotations	1–2 minutes		
2	Cycling (either of the two)			
	Sprint cycling	20 minutes	High	Non-stop
	Long-distance cycling	30–40 minutes	Mild to moderate	Maximum 20 seconds and not more than five times
3	Cool down: Stretches	5 minutes	Mild	

Note: Pump up the music on your earphones and enjoy!

Meal Plans

The exact time of all your meals will depend upon your daily schedule and the time of day you plan to train. Pre-workout snacks can be taken anywhere between one to three hours before training begins. There should be enough time for your stomach to feel comfortable—not too full and not too hungry. The time of the pre-workout snack will, however, depend upon how efficiently you will digest the food. The post-workout meals should ideally be consumed immediately after your workout in order to start the process of refuelling.

Workout Day Meal Plan

Meal 1	Pre-workout	Post Workout	Meal 4	Meal 5
1 cup oatmeal	2 oranges	1 scoop Vitargo or Karbolyn or waxy maize carbohydrates or 1 sachet of gel with water	1 cup cooked brown rice	100 grams fish or 5–6 egg whites
2 whole eggs	½ cup oats	1 scoop whey isolate protein powder	100 grams chicken breast or 150 grams paneer	1 bowl salad drizzled with lemon juice and 1 tablespoon of olive oil or flaxseeds
1 cup skimmed milk	1 scoop whey protein isolate powder	1 scoop BCAAs (you can sip this during the session as well)	1 cup grilled mixed vegetables in 1 tablespoon of olive oil	
1 banana	1 cup unsweetened almond milk			

Non-Workout Day Meal Plan

Meal 1	Meal 2	Meal 3	Meal 4	Meal 5
4–5 egg whites	1 cup all-bran cereal	2 slices whole wheat bread and mustard to taste	100 grams fish	1 cup paneer
2 slices whole wheat toast with 1 tablespoon natural peanut butter	1 banana	150 grams paneer	1 cup steamed sprouts	1 tablespoon walnut pieces
1 orange	1 cup skimmed milk		1 cup cooked brown rice	½ cup strawberries
		Cucumber, lettuce, tomato		
		1 apple		

Swimming
Four Week Workout Plan

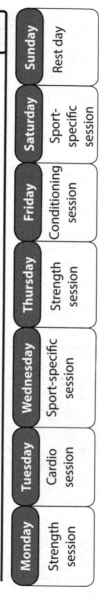

Monday	Tuesday	Wednesday	Thursday	Friday	Saturday	Sunday
Strength session	Cardio session	Sport-specific session	Strength session	Conditioning session	Sport-specific session	Rest day

The tables below provide a broad idea of what each workout session should look like:

Strength Session Workout Plan: The strength training protocols may continue for up to twelve weeks.

Excercise Order	Exercise	Sets	Rest Period	Repetitions					Duration
				Set 1	Set 2	Set 3	Set 4	Set 5	
1	Warm-up: Treadmill or elliptical machine or rowing or cycling								10 minutes
2	Wide grip lat pulldowns: Start with two light warm-up sets	3	60 seconds	10	8	6			Maximum 60 seconds per set
3	Seated dumb-bell shoulder press: Start with two light warm-up sets	3	60 seconds	10	8	6			Maximum 60 seconds per set
4	Barbell bench press	4	60 seconds	12	10	8	6		Maximum 60 seconds per set

Exercise Order	Exercise	Sets	Rest Period	Repetitions Set 1	Set 2	Set 3	Set 4	Set 5	Duration
5	TheraBand raises: lat, front and rear shoulder raises	3	Non-stop	10	10	10			Maximum 60 seconds per set
6	Back squats: Start with two light warm-up sets	4	60 seconds	10	8	6	3		Maximum 60 seconds per set
7	Cool down: Stretches								10 minutes

Note: Increase weights as each set progresses and progressively overload each week by adding 2.5–5 pounds of resistance.

Cardio Session Workout Plan: This is a supplementary workout in order to improve your heart rate for when you're actually playing the sport.

Exercise Order	Exercise	Duration	Intensity	Rest Period
1	Warm-up: Treadmill or spot jogging	10 minutes	Mild	
2	Rowing or cycling	15–20 minutes	Moderate	Non-stop
3	Elliptical cross trainer or swimming	30-45 minutes	Moderate	Non-stop
4	Cool down: Stretching	5 minutes		

Note: Perform this session at a pace of around six to seven on a scale of one to ten, with ten being maximum effort.

Conditioning Session Workout Plan: This session will help improve your conditioning levels.

Excercise Order	Exercise	Sets	Rest Period	Repetitions					Duration
				Set 1	Set 2	Set 3	Set 4	Set 5	
1	Warm-up: Treadmill or elliptical machine or rowing or cycling								5 minutes
2	Skipping	6	30 seconds	20 skips	20 skips	20 skips	20 skips	20 skips	Maximum 60 seconds per set
3	Kettlebell clean and press	5	10 seconds	20	20	15	15	15	Maximum 60 seconds per set
4	HIIT stationary bike		Non-stop						10 minutes
5	Cool down: Stretches								5 minutes

Sports Session Workout Plan: This session is the reason you are doing other workouts and following a nutrition plan. Enjoy this day.

Exercise Order	Exercise	Duration	Intensity	Rest Period
1	Warm-up: Slow-paced swimming laps	1–2 minutes	Leisurely	
2	Swim (either of the two)			
	Sprint swimming	20 minutes	High	Non-stop
	Long-distance swimming	30–40 minutes	Mild to moderate	Maximum 20 seconds and not more than five times
3	Cool down: Stretches	5 minutes	Mild	

Note: Put on a smart swimsuit, feel fit and enjoy the laps!

Meal Plan

Workout Day Meal Plan

Meal 1	Pre-workout	Post Workout	Meal 4	Meal 5
2 whole eggs scrambled with 1 cup diced vegetables	1 banana	1 scoop whey isolate protein powder	1½ cup whole wheat pasta with tomato sauce	100 grams paneer
1 cup oats	¾ cup plain yogurt	1 scoop waxy maize or Karbolyn or 1 sachet of gel with water	100 grams chicken breast	10 almonds
1 banana	½ cup bran cereal	1 scoop BCAAs and a sports drink	1 cup sautéed vegetables—onions, mushrooms, peppers, etc.	

Non-Workout Day Meal Plan

Meal 1	Meal 2	Meal 3	Meal 4	Meal 5
3–4 egg whites	2 slices whole wheat bread	1 apple	1 cup cooked amaranth or 2 amaranth rotis	2 hard-boiled eggs
2 slices whole wheat toast	100 grams white turkey meat	1 cup vegetables	100 grams fish	1 cup diced vegetables
1 tablespoon peanut butter	2 tablespoons flaxseed powder	2 tablespoons hummus	1 cup steamed sprouts	
1 cup watermelon	Salad of cucumber, tomato and lettuce			
1 slice low-fat cheese	1 banana			

Marathon Running
Four Week Workout Plan

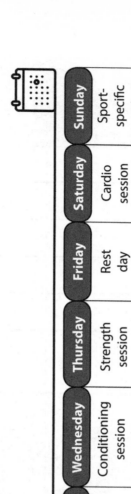

Monday	Tuesday	Wednesday	Thursday	Friday	Saturday	Sunday
Strength session	Sport-specific session	Conditioning session	Strength session	Rest day	Cardio session	Sport-specific session

The tables below provide a broad idea of each what workout session should look like:

Strength Session Workout Plan: The strength training protocols may continue for up to twelve weeks.

Exercise Order	Exercise	Sets	Rest Pertiod	Repetitions					Duration
				Set 1	Set 2	Set 3	Set 4	Set 5	
1	Warm-up: Treadmill or elliptical machine or rowing or cycling								10 minutes
2	Foam rolling (quads or calves or hamstring or IT bands)								10 minutes
3	Circuit 1 i Back squats ii. Barbell bench press iii. Seated dumb-bell shoulder press	3 rounds 3 sets each	Non-stop	15	15	15			Maximum 3 minutes per set

Exercise Order	Exercise	Sets	Rest Period	Repetitions					Duration
				Set 1	Set 2	Set 3	Set 4	Set 5	
4	Circuit 2	3 rounds							
	i. Body weight push-ups ii. Oblique twists iii. Narrow grip cable row	3 sets each	Non-stop	15	15	15			Maximum 3 minutes per set
5	Circuit 3	3 rounds							
	i. Walking lunges ii. Lateral pulldowns	3 sets each	Non-stop	15	15	15			Maximum 3 minutes per set
	iii. Swiss ball crunches			20	20	20			
6	Cool down: Stretches								10 minutes

Note: Increase weights as each set progresses and progressively overload each week by adding 2.5–5 pounds of resistance.

Cardio Session Workout Plan: This is a supplementary workout in order to improve your heart rate for when you're actually playing the sport.

Exercise Order	Exercise	Duration	Intensity	Rest Period
1	Warm-up: Skipping or warm-up swim laps	2–4 minutes	Mild	
2	Swimming or cycling	30–45 minutes	Moderate	Non-stop
3	Cool down: Slow laps in the pool or stretches	5 minutes		

Note: Perform this session at an intensity level of around five to six on a scale of one to ten, with ten being maximum effort.

Conditioning Session Workout Plan: The conditioning session will help boost your performance when you're participating in races.

Exercise Order	Exercise	Sets	Rest Period	Repetitions					Duration
				Set 1	Set 2	Set 3	Set 4	Set 5	
1	Warm-up: Treadmill or elliptical machine or rowing or cycling								5 minutes
2	Box jumps	3	10 seconds	20	20	20			Maximum 60 seconds per set
3	Kettlebell swings	2	10 seconds	20	20				Maximum 45 seconds per set
4	HIIT stationary bike i. 60 seconds full speed ii. 60 seconds moderate recovery speed	15	Non-stop						60 seconds
5	Cool down: Stretches								5 minutes

Sports Session Workout Plan: This session is the reason why you are doing other workouts and following a nutrition plan. Enjoy this day.

Exercise Order	Exercise	Duration	Intensity	Rest Period
1	Warm-up: Slow-paced jog	1–2 minutes	Leisurely	
2	Running	60–90 minutes	Mild to moderate	Non-stop
3	Cool down: Stretches	5 minutes	Mild	

Note: Listen to some peppy music or the sound of waves or just the beating of your heart. Whatever it may be, it's your time to unwind.

Meal Plan

Workout Day Meal Plan

Meal 1	Pre-workout	Post Workout	Meal 4	Meal 5
1 cup of oats (raw measure)	1 whole wheat slice of bread with hummus/mustard/pesto	2 scoops Vitargo or Karbolyn or waxy maize carbohydrates	100 grams tofu	2 tablespoons peanut butter
2 whole eggs and 3 egg whites scrambled with ½ cup vegetables	1 cup skimmed milk	1 scoop whey isolate protein powder	1 cup cooked brown rice	1 cup skimmed milk
1 banana		Electrolyte or sports drink (take after exercise)	1 cup steamed vegetables	1 piece dark chocolate
1 tablespoon peanut butter	1 medium-sized beetroot		½ cup dals	

Non-Workout Day Meal Plan

Meal 1	Meal 2	Meal 3	Meal 4	Meal 5
2 poached eggs	100 grams grilled chicken breast	1 apple	200 grams baked sweet potato	100 grams tofu, thinly sliced and sautéed in a little oil, salt, pepper and spices as desired
2 slices whole wheat toast	1 bajra roti	1 cup vegetables	100 grams chicken	1 slice wholegrain bread
1 cup melon	1 cup steamed sprouts	3 tablespoons hummus	1 cup steamed cauliflower	¼ sliced avocado
1 cup milk	1 peach or kiwi	½ cup plain yogurt		Lemon juice drizzled on top of the avocado

Cricket
Four Week Workout Plan

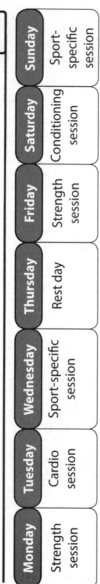

Monday	Tuesday	Wednesday	Thursday	Friday	Saturday	Sunday
Strength session	Cardio session	Sport-specific session	Rest day	Strength session	Conditioning session	Sport-specific session

The tables below provide a broad idea of each workout session should look like:

Strength Session Workout Plan: The strength training protocol may continue for up to twelve weeks.

Excercise Order	Exercise	Sets	Rest Pertiod	Repetitions Set 1	Set 2	Set 3	Set 4	Set 5	Duration
1	Warm-up: Treadmill or elliptical machine or rowing or cycling								10 minutes
2	Back squats: Start with two light warm-up sets	3	60 seconds	10	8	6			Maximum 60 seconds per set
3	Standing overhead press: Start with two light warm-up sets	3	60 seconds	10	8	6			Maximum 60 seconds per set
4	Barbell bench press	4	60 seconds	12	10	8	6		Maximum 60 seconds per set
5	Dumb-bell rows	4	60 seconds	12	10	8	6		Maximum 60 seconds per set

Exercise Order	Exercise	Sets	Rest Period	Set 1	Set 2	Set 3	Set 4	Set 5	Duration
				Repetitions					
6	TheraBand raises: Lateral, front and rear shoulder raises	3	Non-stop	10	10	10			Maximum 60 seconds per set
7	Plate oblique twists (per side)	3	10 seconds	12	12	12			Maximum 60 seconds per set
8	Swiss ball crunches	3	10 seconds	12	12	12			Maximum 60 seconds per set
9	Cool down: Stretches								5 minutes

Note: Increase weights as each set progresses and progressively overload each week by adding 2.5–5 pounds of resistance.

Cardio Session Workout Plan: This is a supplementary workout in order to improve your heart rate for when you're actually playing the sport.

Exercise Order	Exercise	Duration	Intensity	Rest Period
1	Warm-up: Drills and skipping	2–4 minutes	Mild	
2	Burpees	60 seconds		Non-stop
3	Football or treadmill	60–90 minutes	Moderate	
4	Cool down: Stretches	5 minutes		None

Note: You should be working at your maximum intensity level for the burpees and at about six to seven on a scale of one to ten, with ten being maximum effort for a game of football or treadmill session.

Conditioning Session Workout plan: This session will help improve your body's capability to do intense exercises for a longer duration of time.

Excercise Order	Exercise	Sets	Rest Pertiod	Repetitions					Duration
				Set 1	Set 2	Set 3	Set 4	Set 5	
1	Warm-up: Treadmill or elliptical machine or rowing or cycling								5 minutes
2	Box jumps	3	10 seconds	15	15	15			Maximum 60 seconds per set
3	Skipping	10	20 seconds	15 skips	15 skips	15 skips	15 skips	15 skips	Maximum 30 seconds per set
4	Kettlebell swings	5	10 seconds	20	20	20	20	20	Maximum 45 seconds per set
5	HIIT treadmill		Non-stop						15 minutes
6	Cool down: Stretches								5 minutes

Sports Session Workout Plan: This session is the reason you are doing other workouts and following a nutrition plan. Enjoy this day.

Exercise Order	Exercise	Duration	Intensity	Rest Period
1	Warm-up: Slow-paced jog	1-2 minutes	Leisurely	
2	Game of cricket	2 hours	As per inning and your position on the field	
3	Cool down: Stretches	5 minutes	Mild	

Note: Cricket is a group activity, so socialize, chit-chat, play well and may the best side win!

Meal Plan

Workout Day Meal Plan

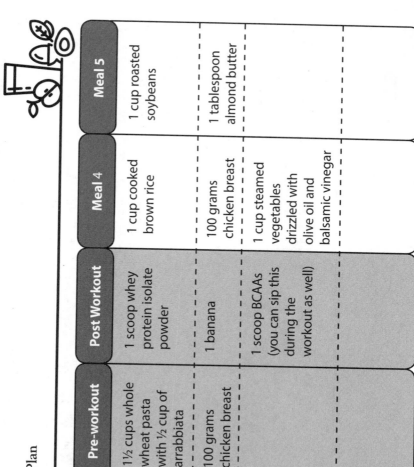

Meal 1	Pre-workout	Post Workout	Meal 4	Meal 5
1 apple	1½ cups whole wheat pasta with ½ cup of arrabbiata	1 scoop whey protein isolate powder	1 cup cooked brown rice	1 cup roasted soybeans
½ cup oats	100 grams chicken breast	1 banana	100 grams chicken breast	1 tablespoon almond butter
1 cup skimmed milk		1 scoop BCAAs (you can sip this during the workout as well)	1 cup steamed vegetables drizzled with olive oil and balsamic vinegar	
2 whole eggs, scrambled with ½ cup vegetables				

Non-Workout Day Meal Plan

Meal 1	Meal 2	Meal 3	Meal 4	Meal 5
2 whole eggs with 2 egg whites scrambled with ½ cup vegetables	100 grams chicken breast	1 apple	100 grams fish	1 cup skimmed milk with unsweetened cocoa
1 whole wheat roti	1 cup cooked brown rice	1 cup plain yogurt	1 cup cooked quinoa or 1 rajgira roti	1 tablespoon flaxseed powder
Spinach leaves, mustard and sliced cucumber as a salad or added to the eggs	½ zucchini grilled with olive oil	2 tablespoons slivered almonds	1 cup bell peppers sautéed in 1 tablespoon olive oil	

There you have it: a broad understanding of sports-specific nutrition and training protocols to help you begin your journey with this new-found love. What I have provided is a one month plan of action, which will need to be upgraded as you progress. Remember progress is subjective. Basically, if two people take up the same sport and nutrition plan, each one of you will show results differently. So don't compare your progress, instead, keep improving on your personal best.

PART VII

A YEAR OF EVENTS

We have chalked out what a typical four-week-long athletic training schedule looks like for each of the commonly played sports, any of which you could decide to play. Let's move forward and talk about the last concept of an athlete's lifestyle: periodization.

18

UNDERSTANDING PERIODIZATION

Periodization is a concept used by almost all athletes, which means looking at your schedule on a much larger scale—often on a yearly basis—and scheduling it accordingly. For instance, let's take a marathoner. During the warmer summer months, they'll be gearing up for peak marathon season. At this point, the primary focus is on optimizing their performance during those marathons and making sure they are well-recovered and nourished.

Prior to this period, they are likely peaking with their training; it will be at an all-time high in order to prepare them for the upcoming events. After the events are finished, they'll take a bit of time away from the sport altogether to let their body recover before training for the next year. When they resume, they'll focus on skill building and strength training to get stronger before sport training ramps up again. This whole cycle is referred to as periodization.

The four phases of periodization that athletes will move through include:

1.   The general preparation phase

2. The specific preparation phase
3. The peaking or the competition phase
4. The recovery phase

If you do decide to eventually take up a sport competitively, or even as a weekend warrior, this concept will work very well for you, allowing you to plan your training around your vacations during off season and a few months in the year as active season. Let's look at each phase individually:

General Preparation Phase

This phase focuses on sport-specific training such as strength training for those who want to get stronger or cross-training exercises for those who need to build cardiovascular endurance. The sport you choose is played twice or thrice a week but definitely not every day.

If you are playing tennis, you need to build more strength by following a specific training schedule and be on a mixed diet of good protein, fat and carbs to fuel your body and achieve this goal. On the flip side, if you want to shed some excess body fat, this may be the right time as sport-specific performance demands aren't very high.

This phase can last anywhere from two to six months, depending on your sport. You'll largely be in this phase through most of the year if you are not a competitive or a recreational athlete. Most of the benefits you'll see will come from this phase.

Specific Preparation Phase

During this phase, the focus is on improving at your sport. At this time, the athlete will likely be spending most of their time working on their sport by doing sport-specific drills.

They'll focus on improving their skills, enhancing their speed, perfecting their technique and so on. Their nutrition needs meet these training demands and because performance is essential, a restrictive diet should be avoided if possible. You need proper fuel to perform and so cutting back your food intake is not recommended.

This phase will typically last another two to five months, depending on your sport and what technique or skills are needed. Considering you may not be competitively involved in a sport, this phase will not last very long. You will probably be able to get actively involved in the preparation phase for a yearly marathon, or club events or a corporate sports day event.

Peaking or Competition Phase

Next comes the peaking or competition phase. This phase represents the peak season in athletics. Basically, this is when you enter competitions, have races and so forth. Physical training is typically reduced slightly during this time (to prevent overtraining and to ensure optimal recovery while going into each event) and is held constant. Performance improvements are not the focus, as the athlete should be trained enough by now such that they are at their very best.

Nutrition should be optimized in this phase. You need to focus on performing optimally—eating well before, during (if applicable) and after training and performing is critical. This phase will only represent a small portion if you choose to compete in an event or race throughout the year.

Recovery Phase

Finally, the last phase is the recovery phase and as the name suggests, this is a time to recover. It's undertaken immediately after peak season. This phase is generally only a few weeks long and is a time of rest and recovery. Light activity may be performed but the goal is not to boost performance.

Nutrition should be high, giving the athlete enough fuel to fully recover from the demanding event they have just completed. For a recreational person, the recovery phase could be your yearly holiday or a few weeks of time off from your monotonous routine.

So there you have a closer look at the concept of periodization. A look at a simple table on the following pages illustrates what the training needs for periodization are for all the sports we have covered in this book. Although I have made some recommendations, the frequency of these sessions can be in accordance with the workout plans suggested earlier.

Sport	Recovery Phase	General Preparation Phase	Specific Preparation Phase	Peaking or Competition Phase
Marathon running	Easy runs and rest	Maintenance running, resistance training, flexibility and agility work	Long runs, tempo runs, easy runs, interval training and maintenance strength training	Easy runs, tempo runs, interval training and running events
Cycling	Easy cycling sessions and rest	Maintenance cycling, resistance training and power training	Long cycling sessions, sprint sessions, tempo sessions, interval training and maintenance resistance training	Easy cycling, interval training and racing events
Racquet sports	Light cardiovascular training and rest	1–2 games per week, cross-training activities, strength training and upper body mobility work	2–3 games/racquet training sessions, maintenance strength training and 1–2 cardio sessions	Games or competitions, 1–2 sport-specific training sessions and cross training

Sport	Recovery Phase	General Preparation Phase	Specific Preparation Phase	Peaking or Competition Phase
Cricket	Light cardiovascular training and rest	Batting or throwing sessions, strength training and cardiovascular training	2–3 games or skill training sessions, maintenance strength training and 1–2 cardio sessions	Games, 1–2 sport-specific training sessions and cross training
Swimming	Easy swims, cycling or jogging and rest	2–3 swimming sessions per week, strength training and mobility training for the shoulders	3–5 swimming workouts and maintenance strength training	Swimming events, easy swims and maintenance strength training

In addition to exercise periodization for various sports, nutrition also varies through the year, complementing the fitness plan of the athlete throughout the training and competitive phase. The table below illustrates the different nutritional requirements of each phase of periodization:

	General Preparation Phase	Specific Preparation Phase	Peaking or Competition Phase	Recovery Phase
Nutrition	Moderate in carbs and fats, slightly higher in protein and maintain or lose body fat	Mixed diet, adequate carbs, protein and fats for post-training recovery and vitamin and mineral supplements to keep immunity and healing processes optimized	High in carbohydrates and low in fats to promote optimal performance and sport-specific, performance enhancing supplements can be included	Easy and comforting diet; eat what you like and enjoy

Training and nutrition will help you achieve your desired goals. But what is also extremely important is being able to prevent injuries, which can be a severe setback to your long and healthy journey into athleticism. Now approaching our final topic of discussion, let's talk about injury prevention.

PART VIII

INJURIES AND INJURY PREVENTION

Nothing is more frustrating than being fully motivated and committed to your training, giving it everything you've got and then getting injured and sidelined as a result. Injuries are a part of progressing with your training. If you learn to not let them bring you down, you have already won the battle for curing yourself.

Let's understand some common injuries, how to prevent them and the various ways to deal with them if they occur.

19

COMMON SPORTS
INJURIES

It's time to talk about one issue that plagues many people as they begin with their sports training: injuries.

If you hope to achieve success, your best bet when it comes to injuries is prevention, because as the saying goes, prevention is better than cure. By understanding what the most commonly experienced injuries are, you can gain a better sense of which ones you may be at risk for and then take steps to overcome them. Let's take a closer look now at these some of these injuries:

Knee Injuries

The first common injury too often experienced is basic knee pain. Knee pain can occur due to a wide variety of different reasons, including poor footwear or equipment, poor muscular strength in the quads and/or hamstrings as well as due to a grinding occurring within the knee joints. Knee pain can also result due to arthritis conditions, which become aggravated as more exercise is performed.

The first step to prevent this injury is to identify whether you are at risk for knee pain in the first place. The questions to ask yourself include:

- Have you suffered from knee pain in the past?
- Do you suffer from arthritis or weak bones?
- Are you playing a high-impact sport (such as running)?

If your answer is yes to any of these three questions, you should always be taking precaution as you are likely on the verge of injury at all times. If you answered no, you should still be aware of knee issues and take steps to prevent them.

Some of the best preventative steps that you can start using, which other top level athletes often use to get around knee injuries, include regular foam rolling of the hip and leg region. This will help release excess tension in the muscle, which could begin to pull at the knee tendons and muscles, resulting in an increased risk of grinding at the knee caps. In addition to this, foam rolling will also help work out any muscle knots, which over time could also increase your risk of knee pain due to tightness and muscle weakness.

What can you do to prevent knee injuries? Here are some steps:

Invest in new shoes at regular intervals

If you are a runner, you must buy new shoes at least twice a year. Even other athletes should be very aware of the mileage they are putting on their shoes (or other footwear they are using) and make sure that they are purchasing new equipment regularly. Remember, even if your shoes look brand new, because you have been training using them frequently, it doesn't mean they are supporting you like new shoes.

Shoes wear out and if they aren't replaced, you won't be getting the support and cushioning that you otherwise would.

Ice your knee

Another smart move is to ice your knee often. If you do a particularly intense session or feel as though perhaps your knee is slightly inflamed, ice it immediately. This is the best way to bring down inflammation, help speed up recovery and reduce the chances that more pain begins to develop. The sooner you can catch an injury that is developing, the better your chances are of avoiding that injury entirely.

Leg strengthening

Finally, the last step to take that will help you defend against knee pain is making sure that you take measures to strengthen the inner and outer thigh muscles along with the quads and hamstrings. For instance, abduction with a resistance band and plies help in increasing flexibility and strengthening of these stiff muscles.

If one of these muscles is stronger than the other opposing muscle, the stronger muscle will begin pulling the knee cap to that side of the knee joint, which then results in experiencing a grinding. This grinding then creates pain and inflammation and soon, you have a full-blown injury.

By making sure to keep all muscles at an even strength level and strengthening them holistically (to help stabilize the knee better), you put your best foot forward at avoiding knee pain.

Back Injuries

The next injury that is very commonly experienced is lower back pain, which is a problematic injury as it'll strike with each and every step that you take, making it very challenging to participate in any sport at all. What's worse is that once you experience back pain, this type of pain is typically chronic in nature, meaning you'll be experiencing it for quite some time to come. The best bet is to avoid it entirely, if at all possible.

Lower back pain, like knee pain, can have many contributing factors. It could be due to lack of strength in the abdominal core, which will cause the lower back to adopt a hyperextended position, which then increases the level of stress placed on the back joints. Similarly, the pain could be due to a high-impact activity. If your body weight is constantly coming down on the spinal column, it causes a high amount of stress that can lead to joint pain.

You may also experience back pain due to an unwanted twist into a natural body position as well. For instance, if you don't have the adequate agility and you move out of proper alignment, it could lead to severe pain.

Back injuries can develop slowly or strike when you least expect it, and so this is one injury to really watch out for.

What can you do to prevent back injuries? Here are some steps:

Strengthen your core

The most important thing you must do to prevent back pain is strengthen your core. Doing so will help ensure that you can easily keep your spinal column in a proper position and that you aren't likely to twist it in an unnatural way. Regular abdominal workouts are critical as is overall strength training for the entire body. Performing heavy squats, deadlifts or lunges will hit all the lower body muscles and strengthen them while also calling the core muscles into play.

If your core is weak, you'll experience decreased overall performance as well as a higher risk of back pain. Core strength training should not be optional for any athlete in training.

Practise proper posture

Ensure that you practise proper posture. Sitting up straight and getting into the habit of doing so will help keep your back muscles stronger, which can help when playing sports. If you often find yourself hunched over your desk while at work or school, this needs to change. Getting into the good habit of using proper posture throughout the day will also increase the chances that you use good posture while participating in your sport as it'll tend to come more naturally.

Ice your back

Once again, using ice is a must. If you are experiencing any sort of lower back pain, ice the area immediately after training. Doing this will keep both the inflammation and swelling down.

Wear proper footwear

Making sure that you have good, supportive footwear is not just important if you are looking to avoid knee pain, but also if you are hoping to avoid back injuries too. Just as your knees need support during high-impact activities such as running, your back joints need similar support as well. Changing your running shoes regularly and making sure that you are wearing the right footwear for your sport in the first place is a must.

Cross train

Finally, the last thing that you can do is making sure that you invest some time in cross training. If you are a marathoner, for instance, a sport where the risk of back pain can be high, consider doing some of your endurance cardiovascular sessions on the bike or elliptical. This will help take some of the impact off those back joints once in a while, allowing for better recovery.

Back pain can also result from simple overuse, so taking steps to allow for adequate rest and recovery will be key.

Tennis Elbow

While tennis forms a part of the name of this injury, it doesn't just happen to those who are playing tennis. It's definitely more common in athletes playing racquet sports, but it can occur in those who are performing regular strength training routines as well.

Tennis elbow is the result of the inflammation of the tendons that surround the elbow and often occurs due to overuse of the muscles in the forearm. Those experiencing this injury will get a nagging and sharp pain when they move their arm in a certain manner or if they lift a heavy object.

Tennis elbow usually develops slowly, so this is one injury that you can actually feel coming on in most cases. If you do, it's time to take steps to heal it immediately. Because tennis elbow can be caused due to overuse, the best way to avoid it is to not use the forearm entirely. Still, this is not a realistic treatment if you are going to continue to play your chosen sport. A better strategy is to first ensure that you have adequate rest and recovery each week to avoid overuse issues in the first place and then put forth a few additional prevention strategies listed below:

Check your form

The very first thing you should do is make sure that you are using good form. Very often, tennis elbow will develop due to using improper form, which places excess strain on the muscles. If you aren't sure if your form is correct, ask a professional to check. You should check your form in both racquet sports as well as any strength training activities you might be doing.

Use a wrap around the elbow

Another thing you might consider doing, either as a preventative strategy or if you start to feel any sort of pain, is using a wrap around the elbow. This wrap will help give the joint extra support and may help take away some of the stress being placed on the tendons and ligaments surrounding the elbow. You will need to wear a wrap on an ongoing basis for it to be effective (or at least while recovering from pain), but it does prove to help many who are suffering.

Note movements that cause pain

Finally, be sure to note movements that cause you a lot of pain. If you find one particular movement is always troublesome, steer clear of that movement as much as possible. For instance, if you are doing a particular strength training exercise that seems too painful, find another way to challenge that muscle. With so many different strength training exercises available, there's no reason you can't find an alternative that won't cause you the issue.

If you do feel any pain developing, make sure that you are icing it immediately to bring down inflammation. It may also be a strong signal that it's time to take a week or two off training and avoid further aggravation.

Tendinitis

Moving along, the next injury that is similar to tennis elbow is tendinitis. This can occur in any joint of the body and is commonly seen in the elbow, shoulder or knee. Swimmers, for instance, are quite likely to suffer from shoulder tendinitis due to the heavy demands that are being placed on their shoulders.

Tendinitis itself is simply the inflammation of the tendons surrounding the joint, typically due to overuse of the joint and/or improper movement patterns. Tendinitis can be quite a nagging injury as well, so it's best to take as many steps as possible to prevent it in the first place.

The best way to prevent this injury?

Treat tendinitis in much the same way as you would deal with tennis elbow. Be sure that you are watching for proper form, using supportive braces if necessary, and allowing for adequate rest and recovery between training sessions. The minute you feel any tendon pain, you should back off training for a few days and treat it accordingly. The sooner you treat it, the greater your chances are for a speedy recovery.

It's those who don't treat such pain and instead let the injury linger for weeks before finally taking time off who suffer the most. At a later point, treatment requires very intensive recovery strategies involving physiotherapy and sometimes even cortisone injections to help bring down the inflammation.

Shin Splints

Shin splits is another common athletic injury as it can occur in any sport where running is done on a regular basis. It is an injury that very often plagues marathoners but it can also strike other athletes, such as those participating in cricket or racquet sports.

Shin splints is usually described as a sharp, intense pain that runs up and down the shins each time the foot strikes the floor. While typically this does occur during running activities, if shin splints is not treated and becomes more severe, it can also occur during walking as well.

Those athletes who are overpronated, meaning they have flat feet with a little arch, tend to be at greater risk of suffering from this condition. It's worthwhile to look at your foot positioning and determine if you need additional support to avoid shin splints.

Those with very flat feet can choose to use a shoe that has a bit more support or may even look into using custom made orthotics to ensure that you are landing on your foot in the most supportive way possible. Here's what can you do to prevent shin splints:

Strengthen your hip and core

The very first thing you want to do is make sure that you are performing regular strength training exercises for the hips and core muscles such as hip bridges, planks and glute contractions. Sometimes, having weak muscles in these areas is one of the biggest contributors to shin splints.

Replace shoes often

Like with knee and back pain, regularly replacing your running shoes will be important in this case as well. If you are running in worn-out shoes, it will not provide the cushion your shins need, leading to jarring pain that travels up and down the leg.

Use a knee sleeve

Some athletes may find it beneficial to wear a knee sleeve around the shin region. This will serve to keep the shin feeling warm and reduce the amount of pain experienced.

Ice your shins

Icing is your best friend with this injury as well. If you feel even the slightest amount of pain, take steps to ice it regularly so that you can reduce inflammation and keep the pain minimal. Don't wait until the injury is full blown to start treating it properly.

Some athletes can get themselves into a situation where shin splints eventually turn into a stress fracture, which will then require much greater care and attention that you'd rather avoid.

With all of these injuries, it should be noted that paying attention to proper warm-up activities is also the key to success. Professional athletes can easily spend twenty to thirty minutes just doing their warm-up, preparing their body for the intense stress that's about to be placed upon them.

While you may not be training at the intensity level of a professional athlete and, therefore, may not need to spend as much time doing your warm-up, you should still never skip it. It will not only get you physically ready to engage in the activity ahead, but will also ensure that you are mentally ready as well.

Now that you have an idea of the most common injuries and how to address and prevent them, let's talk about proper recovery nutrition.

20

NUTRITION FOR HEALING

Picking up a new training regime can sometimes bring along with it unwanted aches and pains. If at any point during these training days you do find yourself in a state of injury and taking time off, don't let this make you believe that you can take a break from focusing on your nutrition. It will be just as important to eat right even now as ever before.

If you don't focus on your nutrition, you could hamper your overall recovery. Remember that your body is in a state of being broken down and needs some raw materials to be able to build itself back up again. If you fail to provide these raw materials, the body simply won't build itself back up as it should.

So what do you need to do for good recovery nutrition? Let's note the key points:

High-quality Protein

The very first thing you want to eat is good quality protein. Your protein needs won't differ too much during recovery as they did while training. You should refrain from bringing your protein intake down because even though you aren't training hard, you'll still be building tissues back up.

Ensure that you focus on taking in high-quality protein often. This means lean chicken, turkey, red meat, fish, eggs and low-fat dairy products, which will provide you with the full spectrum of amino acids you need to rebuild those damaged tissues.

Your other choices of protein are minimally processed meats, eggs, legumes, plant-based proteins and protein supplements. Glutamine is a specific amino acid which successfully helps in tissue repair, and using a supplement of around 10 grams per day for two weeks is a useful addition.

Sufficient Carbohydrates

In addition to protein, you also want to take in a good dose of carbohydrates. Now, you won't need as many carbohydrates as you did while training, as you aren't expending as much energy. That said, resist the urge to cut way back here either. Some athletes fear that they will put on weight if they don't immediately cut their carbs after an injury. This will, in most cases, just halt the entire recovery process. Aim for at least 2 grams per kilogram of body weight, if not slightly more during this time.

What's most important is that you choose which carbohydrates wisely. Whole oats, wholegrains, millets (bajra), sprouted grains (jowar and ragi), bran atta and quinoa are very good choices. Good sources of carbohydrates are also rich in many vitamins. Include brightly-coloured fresh fruit and vegetables (oranges, grapefruits, berries, peppers, broccoli etc.).

Healthy Fats

You also need to make sure that you are tending to healthy fat intake. Like with carbs, don't cut these down too much as your body needs them to stay healthy. You may cut back slightly because you aren't expending as much energy with your training, but do keep them up to a certain level.

In particular, now is the perfect time to really focus on those foods rich in omega-3 fatty acids such as salmon, mackerel, mixed nuts and seeds (particularly flaxseeds and walnuts), avocados and olive oil. These omega fats will help bring down the overall level of inflammation in the body, which is the key to recovery.

Those with high intakes of omega fatty acids may find they experience such great pain relief consuming these alone. They may not need to resort to taking other over-the-counter or prescription pain medications, many of which come with unwanted side effects.

Vitamins, Minerals and Home Remedies

During this time, eating foods rich in vitamins and minerals helps in the post-injury healing process and building good immunity. Rich foods are important as they will help with the production of white blood cells, which are the cells in the immune system that fight against infection and injury.

Around 1–2 grams per day of vitamin C helps to keep your immune system going, which basically helps speed up the recovery process and keeps you healthy overall, while your body is fighting the injury. Focus on carbohydrate sources rich in vitamin A such as carrots, sweet potatoes, pumpkin and spinach. Around 10,000 IU per day for two weeks post injury helps in fast and safe healing.

Around 15–30 mg of zinc will help ensure that your body is able to utilize the protein that you consume to rebuild the tissues, making them stronger and healthier. Food sources rich in zinc include chicken, nuts and seeds.

Age-old home remedies handed down in most families can also help substantially. These remedies include five teaspoons of turmeric powder a day in water or milk or by itself, eating two to four cloves of garlic a day, consuming oranges and pineapples one to many times a day. These fruit and spices help in managing injury-induced inflammation.

Ensure you supplement these foods with plenty of water as well, which will help ensure that your body is running as optimally as possible and rebuilding the tissues at an accelerated rate.

A New Beginning

Hopefully, you now see all the many benefits of introducing athletic training into your lifestyle. You do not need to devote hours and hours a week like competitive athletes do to reap the many benefits that this style of training and nutrition can bring you.

If you want to be a strong, fit and healthy individual, it's this type of training and nutrition that can do that for you. Such training will also help you gain an attractive body that you can feel very proud of.

Those who work hard and put in sustained efforts will see improvements in both their physical capabilities in the sport they choose as well as their day-to-day lives. With all the strength they gain and increase in fitness, they will see a direct transfer over to all the activities they do, thus improving their quality of life.

Athletic training is fun, constantly changing and evolving, and will challenge you in a way that helps you become a stronger person. Just like many other things in life, remember to be patient to see visible results. So keep going till you achieve your fitness targets and hopefully by then, athleticism would have become your new religion.

GLOSSARY

YOUR EXERCISE GUIDE

Back Squats

  i. Target area: Thighs, hips and buttocks
 ii. Starting position: Stand with your feet shoulder width apart, hands in front, stomach in and back straight.
iii. Active movement: Try to sit as low as possible, pushing the buttocks behind with the knees and toes in one line. Stand up to the starting position by using the power from your gluteal muscles (buttocks) and putting pressure on your heels and not toes.

Tip: It's like sitting on a chair—just without a chair! You can use a chair to get the correct posture, making sure you are pushing your butt behind and keeping the back straight. Try and do it in front of a mirror to catch any mistakes.

Barbell Bench Press

i. Target area: Chest
ii. Starting position: Lie back on a flat bench, hold the bar above your chest with your arms locked. Hold the bar with a strong grip slightly wider than your shoulder width.
iii. Active movement: Start bringing the bar down slowly until it touches your middle chest. Pause. Push the bar back up locking your arms. The force should be generated from the chest and not your back.

Tip: Keep the upper and lower back glued to the bench. This way, the power will get generated from the chest muscles.

Body Weight Push-ups

i. Target area: Chest, arms, shoulders and upper back
ii. Starting position: Lie on a mat, face down, palms beside your chest and legs straight.
iii. Active movement: Push yourself away from the floor, using the chest and shoulder muscles. Your entire body is basically on your toes and palms. Go all the way up locking your elbows. Pause and come back to the mat in a controlled manner.

Tip: Try doing push-ups on your knees first if you find it difficult to do it with straight legs.

Box Jumps

i. Target area: Legs
ii. Starting position: Place a stepper or a box in front of you. Start with minimal height of the box till you get the correct posture. Once you are confident, increase the height to an appropriate level (around 1–2 feet).
iii. Active movement: Stand in front of the box, squat and jump up as high as possible and land on the box. Step down and repeat again.

Tip: Swing your arms to get the momentum going. Focus on landing on your heels and not toes.

Burpees

i. Target area: Full body
ii. Starting position: Stand straight, feet shoulder width apart and hands on your side.
iii. Active movement: Sit down into a full squat, place your hands in front of you and jump out throwing your feet behind, thus bringing your body into a push-up position. Keep your core tight and jump your feet back in to stand up straight. Use this momentum and explosively jump up in the air with hands touching the ceiling. Land and get back in to the squat. Repeat.

Tip: Keep the movement quick and explosive to get the heart rate up.

Dumb-bell Row

i. Target area: Back
ii. Starting position: Hold dumb-bells in each hand and bend over with the dumb-bells hanging in front of you in line with the shoulders.
iii. Active movement: Pull the weights straight up to the side of your chest. Squeeze the back muscles and freeze the rest of the body. Pause. Lower the dumb-bell back to the starting position.

Tip: Let only the arms move in this exercise.

High-Intensity Interval Training (HIIT): These are intense bursts of exercise carried out in less than thirty minutes, involving different or the same body parts. HIIT is typically performed with your own body weight or very light weights. This is a fast-paced workout that gets the heart rate shooting up in no time.

Kettlebell Swings

i. Target area: Full body
ii. Starting position: Stand with your feet hip width apart. Grip the kettlebell tightly with one or both hands. Keep knees soft, abs tucked in, shoulders down and chest out.
iii. Active movement: Bend slightly, keep arms long and swing the kettlebell behind from between the thighs like you are going to hit the wall behind. Instantly shift the body weight to the heels and explode through the hips, creating a pelvic thrust, and swing the kettlebell up. Use

the momentum to bend down once again and snap the hips to swing the kettlebell.

Tip: At no point should your lower back hurt. If it does, you are not performing the exercise correctly.

Kettlebell Clean and Press

  i. Target area: Full body
 ii. Starting position: Stand in a partial squat with arms extended downwards, holding the kettlebell with a strong grip.
iii. Active movement: Pull the kettlebell off the floor and instantly raise the kettlebell above your shoulder. At the same time, rotate the grip and let the weight fall on your wrist. Push the kettlebell up for the shoulder press. Stand straight with the elbows locked. Drop the kettlebell forward by rotating the arm with the wrist and moving back into the partial squat position.

Tip: Keep your grip tight while performing this exercise.

Lat Pulldown

  i. Target area: Lats, shoulders, biceps and triceps
 ii. Starting position: Sit down on a pulldown machine, hold the bar above your shoulders, arms locked with a grip wider than shoulder width. Sit upright but slightly away from the central line with your lower back curved and upper chest sticking out.

iii. Active movement: Bring the bar down until it touches your upper chest. Pause. Slowly raise the bar against gravity in a controlled manner to the starting position. Focus on squeezing the back muscles by trying to make the shoulder blades touch each other.

Tip: Don't oscillate your upper body to ease off the shoulders. Freeze your torso and just let the shoulders and arms move.

Narrow Grip Cable Row

i. Target area: Back
ii. Starting position: Hold the handles of the cable machine with a grip narrower than shoulder width. Bend over with your hands hanging in front of you, in line with the shoulders. Keep the torso almost parallel to the ground.
iii. Active movement: With elbows close to the body, pull the rope straight into the side of your chest. Squeeze the back muscles and freeze the rest of the body. Pause. Lower the bar back to the starting position.

Tip: Only the arms should move in this exercise.

Oblique Twists

i. Target area: Abdomen
ii. Starting position: Lie back on a mat, keep the knees bent and feet slightly away from the buttocks.

iii. Active movement: Bring the upper body upwards and create a V-shape with your body. Then twist your torso with the arms touching the floor on the side you are twisting. Come back to the centre and twist on the other side.

Tip: Keep the feet glued to the mat or under a table to get a good grip while twisting.

Plate Oblique Twist

i. Target area: Abdomen
ii. Starting position: Lie back on a mat, keep your knees bent and feet slightly away from the buttocks. Hold the plate with arms straight in front of you and elbows locked.
iii. Active movement: Bring the upper body upwards and create a V-shape with your body then twist your torso with the plate and arms parallel to the floor. Come back to the centre and twist on the other side.

Tip: Keep the feet glued to the mat or under a table to get a good grip while twisting the upper body.

Power Cleans with Standing Calf Raises

i. Target area: Full body
ii. Starting position: Stand in a partial squat with the arm extended downwards, holding the barbell with a strong grip, shoulder width apart.
iii. Active movement: Pull the bar off the floor towards the shoulders with the elbow pointing upwards. Keep the

bar close to your body. Immediately transit into rotating your palms with the elbows pointing downwards and pushing the bar straight up. While the bar is straight up above you, go on to your toes for the calf raise. Slowly get the heels back on the floor and bring the bar back to base.

Tip: Use the momentum of the pulling action to push the bar up.

Rotator Cuff External Rotation

i. Target area: Shoulder
ii. Starting position: At the cable machine, grab the rope horizontally in your left hand, away from the cable machine. The rope should cut you across your torso. Keep your elbow stuck to the waist. Maintain a ninety-degree angle from your elbow at all times. Then switch to the right hand in the same position.
iii. Active movement: Keeping the rest of the body stationary, start moving the cable on the left side only with your wrist outwards as far as you can go, keeping the elbow glued to the waist. Slowly bring it back to the starting position. Repeat the same with your right hand.

Tip: The wrist, arm and elbow should be in a straight line parallel to the floor at all times.

Standing Overhead Shoulder Press

i. Target area: Shoulders

ii. Starting position: Stand holding dumb-bells in each hand with your feet shoulder width apart. Bring the weights to the shoulders with the elbows parallel to the ground and in line with the shoulders.

iii. Active movement: Push the dumb-bells upwards till they touch each other. Lock your arms. Pause. Then bring them down in a controlled manner against gravity back to starting position.

Tip: Hold your abs in and freeze the rest of the body. Only let the arms move. Reduce the weights if you tend to swing your upper body.

Seated Dumb-bell Shoulder Press

i. Target area: Shoulders

ii. Starting position: Sit down on a bench or a Swiss ball or a chair. Hold a dumb-bell in each hand. Bring the weights to the shoulders with the elbows in line with the shoulders.

iii. Active movement: Push the dumb-bells upwards till they touch each other. Lock your arms. Pause. Then bring them down in a controlled manner against gravity back to starting position.

Tip: Hold your abs in and freeze the rest of your body. Only let the arms move. You will feel direct pressure on your shoulders.

Sumo Deadlifts

i. Target area: Legs

ii. Starting position: Keep the feet wide, knees and toes in one line pointing outside. Bend the knees and hips with the arms extended downwards holding the bar.

iii. Active movement: Chest up, face forward, pick up the bar and lean forward driving the hips into the bar. Return the bar back to the ground in a controlled manner.

Tip: Keep your toes and knees in one line at all times.

Superset: All of the above HIIT exercises are to be performed one after the other without rest between them. Take rest after you have performed one set of each exercise and then repeat.

Swiss Ball Crunches

i. Target area: Abdomen

ii. Starting position: Lie back on a Swiss ball with only your lower back supported by the Swiss ball. The rest of the body should be parallel to the ground.

iii. Active movement: Start getting up with your hands behind your neck or straight in front of you. Crunch the ab muscles without moving the ball and keep the feet glued to the floor. Pause. Bring the upper body down and parallel to the ground.

Tip: Keep the neck still at all times.

TheraBand Exercises: These are resistive bands to perform various exercises with mild to moderate resistance. They are a great tool for the recovery and rehabilitation of muscles.

TheraBand Lateral, Front and Rear Shoulder Raises

i. Target area: Shoulders
ii. Starting position: Grasp the ends of the band in both your arms and stand on the centre of the band, thus keeping the band in its position for performing the exercise.
iii. Active movement:
   a. Lateral: Lift the band upward, keeping your elbows straight and thumbs up. Stop at shoulder level. Pause and slowly return to the side of the thighs.
   b. Front: Lift the band in the front with your wrist, arms and shoulders in one straight line. Keeping your elbows locked, pause and slowly return to the front of the thighs.
   c. Rear: Sit on a bench or a chair, bend forward, keep both the arms slightly bent at the elbows, lift the band straight to the side until both arms are parallel to the floor. Hold the position and slowly return.

Tip: Grasp the ends of the band well. Start with an easy band and progress towards a tighter, more resistive band.

Walking Lunges

i. Target area: Legs
ii. Starting position: Place your hands on your hips, feet shoulder width apart, abs tight, back straight and chest out.
iii. Active movement: Place one leg in the front and dip the knee of the back leg down touching the floor. Form a ninety degree angle of both the legs from the knee joint.

Pause. Bring both the feet together and get the next leg forward. Repeat.

Tip: Keep the knee of the front leg in line with the toes at all times. Drive force through the heel of the leading leg to move forward.

Wide Grip Lat Pulldown

i. Target area: Lats, shoulders, biceps and triceps
ii. Starting position: Sit down at a pulldown machine, hold the bar above your shoulders, arms locked and holding the bar as wide as your arms go. Sit upright but slightly away from the central line with your lower back curved and upper chest sticking out.
iii. Active movement: Bring the bar down until it touches your upper chest. Pause. Slowly raise the bar against gravity in a controlled manner to the starting position. Focus on squeezing the back muscles by trying to make the shoulder blades touch each other.

Tip: Don't oscillate your upper body to ease off the shoulders. Freeze your torso and just let the shoulders and arms move.

A NOTE ON THE AUTHOR

 Kinita Kadakia Patel is an award-winning sports nutritionist who works with leading sports teams, organizations and schools. Her clients include numerous national and international athletes, celebrities, models and prominent industrialists. She has an MSc in dietetics with research in sports nutrition, along with certifications from The Oxford College (London), Sports Dietetics Association (Australia) and International Sports Science Association (USA).

Kinita is the founder of MEALpyramid, a Mumbai-based consultancy chain for fitness and nutrition. Besides being a practising sports nutritionist, she is also a lecturer, columnist, fitness enthusiast and mother. She is a marathoner, swimmer and HIIT workout lover—someone who clearly understands her clients' energy needs and demanding schedules, which helps her plan effective nutrition programmes without any compromise on food intake.

For more information, please visit *http://www.mealpyramid.com* and *http://www.kinitakadakia.com*.

DON'T STOP HERE. CONTINUE YOUR JOURNEY. LET'S CONNECT.

Congratulations! By picking up this book you have taken the first step towards bringing out the athlete in you.

An athletic lifestyle is a journey and does not simply end with this book.

I invite you to stay connected with me and others like us on our exclusive discussion forum. On this forum, readers can connect with each other to inspire and be inspired, exchange experiences and share tips.

To sign up, please visit my website *www.kinitakadakia.com* and use the unique code printed below:

TaiyKk321